Introducing
Travel & Tourism

Bob Holland & Ray Youell

t and t publishing
.co.uk

Published by Travel and Tourism Publishing Limited.

www.tandtpublishing.co.uk
info@tandtpublishing.co.uk
www.bobholland.org

© Bob Holland and Ray Youell 2008

First published 2008

British Library Cataloguing in Publication Data is available from the British Library on request.

ISBN 978 0 9550190 7 4

Acknowledgements

Thanks to everyone who provided images for use in this book:

Paul Crick
Jayne Clancy
Darren Leftwich
Clare Holland
Graham Holland
Wendy Holland

Designed and typeset by Sulwyn at Gomer Press
Cover image Bob Holland
Printed in the UK by Gomer Press, Llandysul

Table of Contents

Introduction

This book provides an in-depth introduction to the study of travel and tourism at Level 3 and, as such, it is intended to be used by students and tutors of GCE (AS and A2), BTEC Nationals and OCR National specifications to provide a broad and detailed introduction to the subject of travel and tourism.

Since many students commence their study of travel and tourism at Level 3 with no prior knowledge of the subject at GCSE or through studying other Level 2 qualifications, every effort is made to introduce and explain all of the terms and concepts with which students will be expected to be familiar. These are explained thoroughly and exemplified. The book also includes over 150 images to help provide interest and to illustrate important aspects of the subject area.

The book is designed to support students and tutors who are either preparing for an examination in Unit 1 of the AS Travel and Tourism specification offered by WJEC, AQA, Edexcel and OCR, or who are preparing to produce portfolio evidence for the BTEC or OCR National specifications. The book will also be a useful reference source for students preparing portfolios covering the development and structure of the United Kingdom travel and tourism industry or sustainable tourism.

The book is divided into the following sections:

Section 1 – The nature of travel and tourism
This section considers the main types of tourism in relation to the United Kingdom. It also examines the motivating and enabling factors relating to tourism. Additionally, this section considers the issues relating to defining tourism.

Section 2 – The characteristics of travel and tourism
This section introduces the range of commercial and non-commercial organisations which make up the travel and tourism industry. The products provided by the industry and the external pressures on the industry are also considered in detail. The role of technology within the industry is also covered.

Section 3 – The structure of the UK travel and tourism industry
In this section, the sectors of the travel and tourism industry are considered in turn, with comprehensive coverage throughout.

Section 4 – The development of the UK travel and tourism industry
This section deals with the development of the United Kingdom travel and tourism industry since the 1930s – from Billy Butlin to Virgin Galactic! The section also includes comprehensive coverage of the impacts of tourism and introduces the concept of sustainable tourism.

Industry Info....
These are snippets of case study information illustrating points made. Many have website addresses from where students and tutors can obtain further information.

Exam preparation
These appear at the end of each topic and set students a range of questions similar to those that could appear in external examinations set by Awarding Bodies.

Glossary
A range of standard terms appropriate to the study of travel and tourism at this level.

Section 1

The nature of travel and tourism

What you will study in this section

1.1 The main types of tourism

1.2 The reasons why people travel

1.3 Defining tourism

Introduction

Travel and tourism is often referred to as the 'world's largest industry' and the 'world's fastest-growing industry'. It is also a very dynamic industry which has had to respond to a wide range of factors outside its control. In the last decade, the growth of international terrorism, the increased use of the internet and other forms of technology to book flights and accommodation, and the growing awareness of climate change, as well as the environmental impact of increased air travel, have all affected the way in which the travel and tourism industry operates.

At the same time, a number of social changes have been taking place. People are living longer and more active lives. Increasing numbers of young people are taking some form of gap year to experience other environments and cultures. It is estimated that about 10 per cent of outbound tourism from the UK is connected with gap year travel. Also, more British people are buying properties in various areas within mainland Europe and are living overseas for part of the year. Areas of southern Europe, such as parts of Spain and the eastern Mediterranean, are becoming more popular in the winter months because they are too hot for some visitors in the summer.

We are increasingly aware of the impacts that tourism has on destinations – both on the people living in those destinations and the natural environment. The need to develop tourism in a sustainable manner is now understood and appreciated by governments and the tourism industry alike. Tourists are increasingly aware of the need to behave responsibly in destination areas, in order to reduce their harmful impacts and make a positive contribution to the economy and culture of holiday areas.

Traditional beach holidays are becoming less popular as more travel choices become available

More young people are taking gap year trips to exotic destinations

international visits for business and leisure purposes throughout their lifetime.

Travel between member countries of the European Union is increasingly common and many of these countries now share the same currency, the Euro. Today, more high-speed trains cross international boundaries

Fewer British people are choosing the traditional package holiday to coastal destinations in Europe. Today, more people are aware of the potentially damaging effects of too much sun than they were a decade ago. The desire for a healthy tan has to be balanced against the risks of contracting skin cancer and other diseases from too much exposure to strong sunshine.

Nearly everyone living in the UK will be a tourist in one form or another. Many people will make a number of

Large numbers of apartments and villas are being built in areas such as the coastal region near Malaga in southern Spain

than in the past and budget airlines have revolutionised short-haul air travel. At the same time, increasing numbers of people from countries such as India and China can afford to take international holidays and these countries will become very important markets in the near future.

Therefore, we can be sure of two things. Firstly, the world of travel and tourism is ever-changing and, secondly, everyone will be part of this world in some way or another throughout their lives. In fact, it is very unlikely that any reader of this publication has not been on holiday or travelled any distance outside of their home town or area where they live.

The purpose of this unit is to help the reader understand the main types of tourism, the reasons why people travel and to investigate just what is meant by 'tourism'.

Cruise holidays have become increasingly popular over the last decade

1.1 The main types of tourism

There are a number of ways in which tourists can be categorised. One of the most common is to identify domestic, inbound and outbound tourists.

- Domestic tourism – people taking holidays, short breaks, business trips and day trips within their own country;

- Incoming (inbound) tourism – this is a form of international tourism involving people travelling into a different country from where they usually live for a holiday or other tourism purpose;

- Outbound tourism – this is also international tourism and involves people leaving the country in which they usually live to take a holiday or other trip abroad.

Domestic tourism in the UK

It is important to understand that tourism does not only involve people from the UK going abroad for holidays. In the past, the majority of tourist activity was domestic and most people have only been able to afford holidays abroad for the last 50 years or so. The traditional British seaside resorts, such as Blackpool, Brighton and Bournemouth, developed to cater for domestic tourists and still rely heavily on UK visitors for their income. When, just before and after the Second World War, holiday camps were developed in the UK near seaside resorts by Billy Butlin and other entrepreneurs, virtually all of their customers were domestic tourists.

Blackpool is a good example of a traditional resort which relies heavily on domestic tourism. Traditionally, Blackpool attracted tourists who enjoyed the beach, amusements and walks along the promenade. Many of these visitors were families and are sometimes referred to as the 'bucket and spade' brigade. These customers were happy to stay in hotels and guesthouses and spend much of their time on the beach. Over time, the resort developed a wider range of activities and attractions such as Blackpool Tower and the illuminations, which were operated late in the season to attract visitors back to the resort outside peak holiday times.

Blackpool beach, Tower and the Pleasure Beach attraction

Many of Blackpool's traditional customers have now decided to take holidays elsewhere. In response, the resort has attempted to cater for different markets. New attractions, such as the Pleasure Beach and Sea World have been developed and a number of small casinos have been opened. The resort also aims to attract short break visitors rather than the traditional week-long tourists and is popular with stag and hen parties.

Much of Blackpool's accommodation is low-priced small hotels and guest houses

The majority of Blackpool's visitors are still domestic tourists, including business tourists who make use of the extensive conference facilities in the resort.

Short breaks are becoming an increasingly popular form of domestic tourism. As increasing numbers of British people take their main holiday abroad, it is becoming more common for those who can take a second or even third holiday a year to take a domestic break, for a weekend or less than a week.

A short break is normally taken for two to four nights and so it is not usually practical to travel internationally. Seaside resorts and historic cities such as Bath and Chester rely heavily on short break domestic tourists.

Domestic holidays have many advantages for tourists. They are generally cheaper because there is less travel involved. Most domestic holidays involve travel by road, although nowadays it is not unusual to fly between domestic destinations and trains are also a popular travel option. Flights between cities such as Belfast, Edinburgh, London and Cardiff may offer the most convenient method of travel for domestic tourists. Visits within the UK are also popular with car drivers who do not feel confident about driving on European roads.

The historic and cultural attractions of Bath are popular with short break domestic tourists

Domestic tourists might choose to stay on a campsite or in a caravan and there are numerous camping and caravan sites throughout the UK. Holidays in caravans are very popular, while other self-catering options, such as holiday cottages and apartments, are also available.

Some tourists are less adventurous than others and feel more confident with their own language, food and culture. Others may feel that there is a greater risk of

9

Static caravans or 'mobile homes' are found at many seaside towns

being involved in terrorist activity or the victim of crime in other countries, so choose to holiday within the UK.

There is a wide range of activity holidays available within the UK. Activities like cycling and walking in National Parks and other countryside areas are extremely popular, often taken as short breaks.

There are a lot of reasons why people take domestic holidays within the UK, but holidays are not the only type of domestic tourism. Many families get together at certain times of the year for festivals and family events. This may well involve some members of the family travelling and staying away from home, making them tourists. Technically, they are said to be 'visiting friends and relatives' (VFR), which is one of the main reasons why people take part in tourist activities.

Domestic tourism also covers more than people taking holidays and short breaks. Throughout the year many

events take place all over the country which encourage people to travel or stay away from home. Major events like the Edinburgh Festival attract thousands of domestic visitors to the city each summer. Exhibitions like the Ideal Home Exhibition in London and a number of events at the National Exhibition Centre in Birmingham also attract visitors who may stay in the area for one or two nights.

Cycling is an active domestic holiday

Music festivals and concerts, like Glastonbury and the Reading Festival, all attract large numbers of people, many travelling from other parts of the country and often camping on site – these are domestic tourists as well.

Additionally, sporting events create domestic tourism. Some people need to stay close to the venues of major sporting events because it is not possible for them to get home after the event has finished. Rugby internationals, football matches and major motor racing events, amongst others, all attract many thousands of spectators, some of whom stay at least one night while attending the event. The next Ryder Cup golf tournament is to be held in Wales in 2010 and already many hotels and other accommodation near the Celtic Manor Resort, which is hosting the event, are fully booked. This will also be the case for accommodation near to designated Olympic venues in London in 2012.

Many sporting events cause people to travel outside of their home area and can be classified as being part of the travel and tourism industry. Some fans are willing to travel long distances at the weekend to support their teams, thereby contributing to the UK tourism economy.

Industry Info...

The Millennium Stadium

The stadium was constructed for the 1999 Rugby World Cup and has become a symbol of modern Cardiff. As well as rugby, the stadium has hosted the FA Cup final and other important football matches for the years when Wembley Stadium was being redeveloped. Additionally, the stadium has now become a popular concert venue with a number of rock bands and artists playing to crowds of more than 40,000. The Millennium Stadium is a major visitor attraction as well, with tours of the stadium's facilities being available. There is no doubt that the stadium has been a major contributor to the recent growth of tourism to Cardiff.

www.millenniumstadium.com

The Millennium Stadium in Cardiff hosts major sporting events and concerts, for which some visitors require accommodation close to the stadium

Away supporters travel outside of their home area and contribute to the tourism economy by travelling on trains and coaches to matches

Travelodges are part of a hotel chain

Domestic tourism also includes business travel. On any mid-week evening and sometimes at weekends, thousands of British people are staying away from home to carry out their work. They may be attending conferences, perhaps staying away for two or three nights, or they may be attending meetings which only require them to be away from home for one night. Business tourism also includes the many people who travel to different parts of the UK on day visits, not involving an overnight stay. It is important to remember that not all business travellers stay in business class hotels with high-class facilities. In the last decade, budget hotels have become extremely popular and these cater well for people travelling on business, as well as leisure customers.

Marriott Hotels cater for both business and leisure visitors

Exam preparation

1. Outline the reasons why people take domestic holidays in the United Kingdom.

2. Discuss the advantages of taking domestic holidays.

3. Explain how visits to sporting events contribute to the tourist economy.

Inbound tourism to the UK

It is important to appreciate that the UK is an important destination in world tourism, attracting tourists from many countries for a variety of reasons. Each day, visitors arrive in Britain from many destinations around the world. Many of these visitors are on holiday or visiting friends and relatives, while others are on business trips. Some arrive from short-haul destinations by air, while others may fly for nearly 24 hours from Australia or New Zealand. Some inbound tourists travel to the UK by ferry and enter the country at a ferry port, while others travel by train and arrive by Eurostar.

Industry Info...

The number of tourists entering each county is carefully monitored. In the United Kingdom, this data is shown in the International Passenger Survey.

The approximate numbers of tourists arriving in the United Kingdom in 2005 were:

By air – 22,000,000
By sea – 4,700,000
By tunnel – 3,250,000
Total arrivals – 30,000,000 (approx)

Purpose of visit:
Holiday – 9,700,000
Business – 8,170,000
Visiting Friends and Relatives – 8,690,000
Other reasons – 3,401,000
Total visits – 30,000,000 (approx)

Adapted from International Passenger Survey data

London is one of the most important tourist cities in the world

The importance of the UK as a destination for inbound business visitors should not be under-estimated. London is one of the most important financial centres in the world. Each working day, business people from Europe, North America and other parts of the world arrive in London for a number of work-related purposes.

Industry Info...

It is also useful to know the origin of inbound tourists to the UK.

Number of visits made to the United Kingdom in 2005 by country of residence:

1	USA	3,438,000
2	France	3,324,000
3	Germany	3,294,000
4	Irish Republic	2,806,000
5	Spain	1,786,000
6	Netherlands	1,720,000
7	Belgium	1,112,000
8	Poland	1,041,000
9	Canada	796,000
10	Sweden	728,000

Adapted from International Passenger Survey data

If these figures were to be examined in more detail, they would show different patterns in terms of the purpose of visit between various countries. For example, it may be that a higher proportion of visitors from the Irish Republic are visiting friends and family, whereas more inbound visitors from Canada are on holiday.

Many inbound business tourists make their way to the City of London where lots of international companies have offices

The popularity of the UK with inbound tourists

Why is the UK so popular with inbound tourists? There are many answers to this question, including:

- Britain has many cultural and historic attractions dating from various periods of history.

- London is one of the most important tourist cities in the world, with a wide range of international attractions. People are particularly attracted by the heritage associated with the Royal Family. Also, London is one of the world's financial capitals, stimulating much business tourism.

- There is a wide variety of landscapes, ranging from the wild upland areas of Scotland to the gentle rolling hills of southern England. Some landscape features, such as The Giant's Causeway and the Lake District, are well known internationally.

The landscape of Dartmoor National Park has a number of 'tors' which attract tourists

- Many towns and villages are seen as being quaint and traditional to inbound tourists.

Villages along canals often provide accommodation and catering facilities for tourists

- The industrial heritage of the UK is increasingly seen as being attractive to visitors.

- The coast of Britain is varied and provides opportunities for a range of tourist activities.

There are many scenic areas along the coastline of Britain

- Stately homes and castles of historic importance attract many visitors from overseas. Additionally, some of these have been used as the setting for films in recent years, for example the Harry Potter films were made at Alnwick Castle in Northumberland.

Longleat in Wiltshire is typical of the English stately home which inbound tourists like to visit

- Towns and areas of countryside are associated with world-famous authors. For example, Stratford-upon-Avon is associated with William Shakespeare and West Yorkshire with the Bronte sisters.

In addition, the UK is generally viewed as a safe destination for inbound tourists, despite current fears about terrorist activity. Also, English is an international language, so North American visitors have confidence in being able to converse with local people. Many visitors from European countries are also able to speak English.

What factors might cause a reduction in the number of inbound visitors to the UK over time?

- Changes in the values of currency (exchange rates) – a rise in the value of the pound sterling would mean that visitors from the USA and Europe might find the UK more expensive and be less likely to visit.

- Terrorist activity – more terrorist threats may cause potential tourists to become cautious and less confident about travelling to and within the UK.

- Bad publicity – events such as the outbreak of foot and mouth disease (FMD), resulting in the closure of parts of the countryside, may deter tourists.

- Increased taxation – more taxes on air travel will add costs to people's holidays and may make them think twice about visiting the UK.

- Poor service levels – if the UK were to get a reputation for poor levels of customer service and is not seen as providing good value for money, inbound tourists may choose other destinations.

Outbound tourism from the UK

UK residents made over 66 million visits abroad in 2005. This could mean that everybody went abroad at least once. In reality, some people make two or more outbound visits a year and some UK residents do not travel abroad at all. About two-thirds of the visits made are for holidays – the rest are for business purposes and for visiting friends and relatives.

Within the category of trips made by people on holiday, there is a variety of types of holiday being undertaken. A significant number of outbound tourists are taking the traditional package holiday to a Mediterranean coastal resort, although the number of these holidays is now in decline.

Some people are taking short breaks to European cities such as Prague, Paris and Barcelona. This has become a popular option with many UK residents and the choice of city breaks has grown with the availability of budget

The Nou Camp Stadium is a popular attraction for many visitors to Barcelona

Industry Info...

Number of visits made by United Kingdom residents by region and purpose of visit in 2001 and 2005

Destination	2001	2005
North America		
Holiday	2,779,000	2,959,000
Business	834,000	855,000
Visiting friends and relatives	947,000	936,000
Other	97,000	120,000
Total	**4,656,000**	**4,869,000**
Europe		
Holiday	32,197,000	36,180,000
Business	6,731,000	6,782,000
Visiting friends and relatives	5,267,000	7,229,000
Other	3,378,000	2,647,000
Total	**47,573,000**	**52,838,000**
Other Countries		
Holiday	3,694,000	5,036,000
Business	655,000	919,000
Visiting friends and relatives	1,514,000	2,483,000
Other	189,000	296,000
Total	**6,052,000**	**8,734,000**
Total World		
Holiday	36,670,000	44,175,000
Business	8,220,000	8,556,000
Visiting friends and relatives	7,727,000	10,648,000
Other	3,664,000	3,063,000
Total	**56,281,000**	**66,441,000**

Adapted from International Passenger Survey data

air travel provided by easyJet, Ryanair and other airlines. Barcelona has become a particularly popular destination for city breaks because of the variety of attractions which meet the needs of a range of tourist groups. It is also accessible from a number of regional airports in the UK. In addition, the city is served by three airports, two of which are used by Ryanair and one by easyJet, making it easy and relatively cheap for visitors to fly from their local airport in the UK.

Another consequence of the growth in air travel to Europe in recent years has been the increase in second homes owned by UK residents, particularly in areas of France and Spain, as well as in other European countries. More people are finding that they are able to afford to buy a house, villa or apartment in a region they have previously visited on holiday.

Air travel is not the only method of transport available for outbound holidays from the UK to Europe. Ferry crossings are available from a number of ports, allowing outbound tourists to travel to their destination by car or in some cases, train. Holidays taken on campsites, or made by touring caravan, are also a popular option. Other outbound tourists choose to drive to a range of destinations throughout Europe.

Not all outbound tourists use accommodation for their visit. Day trips to France for shopping or sightseeing are popular with people living close to Channel ports. This is sometimes referred to as a 'booze cruise' because many people bring a supply of alcoholic drinks back into the UK. Such people are counted as international tourists, but return to their home in the evening.

Buying a second home abroad, such as an apartment near the coast in Spain, has become affordable and fashionable

New York is a popular destination and short break shopping trips have become a favourite

Over the last twenty years, the number of outbound visits from the UK to destinations outside of Europe using long-haul flights has increased rapidly. The first destination to become popular was Orlando in Florida, because of the famous Disney attractions. Other destinations in the United States of America have also increased in popularity. Prices of flights to America are relatively much cheaper now, with a number of daily scheduled services to many US cities.

Finally, UK residents have been able to travel further in recent years. Long-haul flights to a multitude of destinations have become more affordable and more UK residents are choosing to visit exotic destinations, such as parts of Asia which were inaccessible in the past.

The Great Wall of China is now more accessible to UK tourists

Exam preparation

1. Outline the reasons why the United Kingdom receives so many inbound tourists.

2. Explain why there has been a growth in outbound tourism in recent years.

3. Analyse the factors which may cause a down turn in the number of tourists visiting the United Kingdom in the near future.

1.2 The reasons why people travel

We discussed in section 1.1 that there are many different reasons why people travel. The travel and tourism industry is about far more than just providing holidays for people – it also includes travel for a variety of other purposes.

It is generally accepted that there are three main reasons for travel. These are:

- Leisure tourism;
- Visiting friends and relatives;
- Business tourism.

Leisure tourism

Leisure tourism includes many of the activities that people think of as 'tourism', such as taking holidays and short breaks. The vast majority of leisure tourist trips can be placed into one of these categories, but additional terms are also sometimes used, including:

- Health tourism – going to a different country to have an operation or medical treatment that is not available or is more expensive in the country where the person usually lives. Also, it is quite common for people to travel in order to convalesce or recover after a period of illness or an operation;
- Educational tourism – school and college visits and foreign language exchanges linked directly to study experiences. Also, some university students may spend an extended period of time on a research project away from home;

- Dark tourism – this is recognised as travel to sites associated with death, torture and disaster. Visits to attractions such as the London Dungeon, the Nazi concentration camps in Europe or even Ground Zero in New York come under this category.

Visits to the sites of concentration camps are part of 'dark tourism'

Holidays

Many leisure tourism trips are taken where the main purpose is relaxation, rest and enjoyment. Such trips are called holidays.

Most holidays are taken in family groups, as couples or with groups of friends. Occasionally, people may choose to go on holiday by themselves for solitude or perhaps to meet new friends. The majority of holidays last less than two weeks. In the early days of domestic tourism nearly all holidays lasted one week – the holiday started and ended on a Saturday.

Industry Info...

Some destinations are increasingly promoting themselves as health or medical tourism destinations. One of these is the Mediterranean island of Malta. The island has been associated with health and wellness since Roman times and today boasts a large number of private hospitals and clinics equipped with state-of-the-art equipment, highly-qualified medical practitioners and a number of facilities for recuperation and rehabilitation. These facilities, together with Malta's warm climate and extensive tourist facilities, make it an ideal destination for health or medical tourism. In January 2008, the Medical Travel Business Congress 2008 was held in Malta.

www.medicalmalta.com

Holidays to beach resorts on the Mediterranean coast are often sold as package holidays

More recently, holidays of two and three weeks have become common and some holidays may even last several months. Short breaks of less than one week are becoming increasingly popular as second holidays. Generally, trips away from home for more than one year are not considered to be holidays.

Holidays can also be classified in terms of how the holiday was purchased. Package holidays are those sold as a 'package' by a tour operator, often through a travel agent. The package would include flights, accommodation and transfers. Independent holidays are arranged by tourists buying flights, accommodation and other travel products without using tour operators. The internet has made this type of holiday a more popular option in recent years.

Other forms of leisure tourism

There are a number of other reasons why people travel for leisure purposes other than for rest and relaxation. These reasons include:

- Health and fitness – such as a cycling tour, rock-climbing trip or a walking holiday;
- Sports – sports tours can be taken as a spectator, such

as a visit to a major sporting event like a motor racing Grand Prix in another country, or they can be taken as a competitor, perhaps running in an athletics meeting, which may entail a stay away from home in the UK or abroad;

- Culture and religion – such as attending a religious festival or service;
- Spiritual and social – such as a meditation course, a retreat or a singles holiday.

Leisure tourism where there is a specific purpose for a visit, rather than just rest and relaxation, is often referred to as activity holidays or special interest holidays. In this type of holiday, the people involved spend a large part of their time involved in a particular activity, which may be related to sport, health, culture or nature, such as a bird-watching holiday.

Skiing and other winter sports can be referred to as special interest or activity holidays

It is important to understand that by no means all leisure tourism is related to rest, relaxation and enjoying the sunshine and nightlife of a Mediterranean resort. People travel away from home to take part in a wide range of leisure tourism activities which may be cultural, spiritual or sporting.

Business tourism

The importance of business tourism to the travel and tourism industry should not be under-estimated. Although leisure tourism is seasonal, business tourism takes place throughout the year and some travel and tourism businesses, such as budget hotel chains, rely heavily on the income from business travellers.

The table on the next page clearly shows the importance of business tourism in terms of outbound tourism. Business tourism also makes an important contribution to domestic tourism, while many tourism authorities are keen to promote the UK as an inbound destination for business tourists.

It is also wrong to assume that all business tourists travel in 'business class' on flights and stay in expensive hotels. All travel involving a stay away from home in connection with someone's job is classed as business travel. This will include workers on a construction project, teachers attending a training course or a group of technicians attending a conference.

Business tourism encompasses a number of different activities including:

1. Business meetings – every day people travel to business meetings. These may or may not involve a stay away from home. Even when business people travel to a

Industry Info...

The number of visits abroad made by United Kingdom residents between 2001 and 2005

Purpose of visit	2001	2002	2003	2004	2005
Holiday	36,670,000	39,902,000	41,197,000	42,912,000	44,175,000
Business	8,220,000	8,073,000	7,892,000	8,140.000	8,556,000
Visiting friends and relatives	7,727,000	7,870,000	8,527,000	9,799,000	10,648,000
Other reasons	3,664,000	3,532,000	3,807,000	3,343,000	3,063,000

Adapted from International Passenger Survey data

meeting and back home the same day, they will make use of the products and services of the travel and tourism industry. Most flights leaving the UK in the morning bound for Paris, Rome or Brussels are carrying business passengers who have to attend meetings in these cities, returning home the same evening. Many motorway journeys or rail journeys are made by people attending business meetings, while hotels close to motorways and railway stations are regularly used by business travellers. Although modern technology such as e-mail and video conferencing are available, people still like to meet face-to-face to discuss important issues and contracts.

2. Exhibitions and trade fairs – many industry sectors have annual exhibitions or trade fairs which attract thousands of visitors. Companies pay to have a stand or display at the exhibition to show off their products to customers. Business people also take the opportunity to hold meetings and make new contacts. Events such as the Motor Show and the Ideal Home Exhibition are long-standing examples of trade fairs and the largest event for the travel industry is the World Travel Market which takes place in London each autumn. Major venues for holding trade fairs in the UK include Earls Court in London and the National Exhibition Centre (NEC) in Birmingham.

3. Conferences and conventions – a wide range of organisations hold an annual conference or convention which may be attended by hundreds of people, many of whom will need to travel and stay away from home for a number of nights. The political parties in the UK usually hold their conferences in seaside resorts during

Exhibitions such as car shows involve people in setting up and running the stands

autumn when the holidaymakers have gone home. Brighton, Bournemouth and Blackpool are commonly used because of specialist venues for holding conferences and the resorts have plenty of suitable hotel accommodation available.

4. Incentive travel – this type of business tourism is often a reward for people who have performed well at work. This might be a week's holiday as a reward for meeting a sales target or for completing a project ahead of schedule. Essentially, employees are rewarded with a free holiday rather than with cash. The holiday is a prize or incentive for working hard.

5. Corporate hospitality – it is becoming increasingly common for companies to entertain their guests while they are visiting on business. For example, companies could entertain visitors from overseas by providing tickets for a major sporting event. Some companies might hire an executive box at a football or rugby match to entertain their guests who are on a business visit.

Business tourism is not all about business! While on a business visit, many people will want to take the opportunity to visit the major attractions in a city or area and may build some time for leisure tourism into their visit. Alternatively, they may not eat in the hotel where they are staying but sample local culture and entertainment. All such visits contribute to the tourism economy of the destination visited.

Corporate hospitality includes providing tickets to customers for major events such as the Rugby World Cup

Business travellers to New York may well find time to visit major attractions such as the Empire State building

Differences between business travel and leisure travel

There are some important differences between business and leisure travel which should be considered.

- More business travellers travel on their own, whereas leisure travellers are more likely to travel in groups;
- More business travel is booked at short notice, whereas most leisure travel is booked some way ahead;
- The business traveller is more inclined to work during the journey, whereas leisure travellers are more likely to enjoy the scenery or entertainment on the journey, such as films on a flight;
- More business travel occurs during weekdays, whereas weekend travel is more popular with leisure travellers;
- In the past, business travel was booked through specialist business travel agencies. Although these still exist, business travellers can also use web-based travel companies today;
- Business travellers are more likely to be experienced travellers and know their way around airports and other facilities, whereas leisure travellers are more likely to be less confident;
- Business travellers do not always travel business class, but some leisure travellers do!

Visiting friends and relatives (VFR)

Of some 66 million outbound tourism trips made from the UK in 2005, over 10 million were for visiting friends and relatives. Add to this the number of visits made by domestic tourists for family events, celebrations or just spending a weekend visiting, and the true value of VFR tourism can be appreciated.

These tourists do not contribute as much to the tourism economy because they tend not to stay in hotels, but they do spend money on a range of products and services provided by the travel and tourism industry. They have to travel to the area where their friends or family live; this might involve a flight, car journey or rail travel. They tend to visit attractions while they are on the visit and they may well visit nearby restaurants to eat and use local transport services.

The people hosting friends and family members are also likely to take part in travel and tourism activities while they have guests staying with them. They may well join their family members on visits to attractions or visit nearby tourist destinations, making use of transport facilities. The families and friends may also eat out together in restaurants. VFR tourism is an area which illustrates how difficult it can be to calculate the precise value of tourism to an area.

A picnic is a popular activity when visiting family and friends

Motivating and enabling factors

People are motivated to take part in tourist activities for a variety of reasons, as the following parts of this section explain.

Motivating factors

Generally, people take part in tourist activities because they choose to. The exception to this is business tourism where, in many cases, people have to attend conferences and meetings, but even here there may be an element of choice involved. Motivational factors are aspects which give people the desire to travel and make choices about the places they wish to visit. 'Wanderlust' is the name which has been given to people's desire to experience different places and cultures. This may be stronger in some people than others.

Many people have a list of destinations they would like to see and experience when they get the opportunity. Some young people make a positive choice not to go into a job before they have travelled to exotic destinations such as Asia and New Zealand to experience different cultures and environments.

For other people, the desire to travel to warmer climates where hot, sunny conditions can be guaranteed is a strong motivational factor. This 'sunlust' is one reason why tourists leave the UK for Mediterranean resorts each summer, because they are far more likely to have settled sunny weather in which to relax on a beach or by a hotel pool. Alternatively, people may be motivated by the need to experience different cultures and head towards museums, art galleries and sites of religious interest. Some people may wish to 'travel in style' and be motivated to stay in

An elephant ride through a tropical forest may be a once-in-a-lifetime activity

Industry Info...

The Adventure Company is one of a growing number of tour operators specialising in providing experiences for those looking for adventure on holiday. The company's website demonstrates the range of options available by stating that 'from kayaking in Croatia and SCUBA diving in Turkey to white water rafting in Nepal and mountain biking in the Pyrenees, we have a whole range of trips designed to get the adrenaline pumping. Many contain a range of different activities throughout the trip so you get to take on a new challenge every day'.

The activities offered by The Adventure Company include:

- Cycling
- Desert Experience
- Rafting and Canoeing
- Rainforest Experience
- River and Sea Journeys
- Safari
- Tribal and Ethnic Encounters
- Trekking
- Wilderness and Wildlife

www.theadventurecompany.co.uk

quality hotels, travel first class where possible and visit destinations which have a certain 'up-market' prestige. Examples of up-market, prestigious destinations are St Tropez and Monte Carlo on the Mediterranean coast. Very often tourists are motivated by the need to relax and to spend quality time with family and friends away from the normal routine of work and home life. Part of the pleasure of tourism is looking forward to the trip or holiday.

One interesting way of putting tourists into groups in terms of motivation is to identify:

>**A**drenaline junkies;
>**B**each bums;
>**C**ulture vultures.

- Adrenaline junkies – seek adventures and excitement from tourism and want to be climbing mountains, skiing on glaciers, hang-gliding, abseiling, bungee-jumping etc.

Abseiling down a waterfall is fun for some people!

'Culture vultures' would enjoy watching local craftsmen at work

'Beach bums' enjoy lazing on a beach

- Culture vultures – enjoy experiencing the local culture, life style and customs of the destination they are visiting. These people are more likely to attempt to learn some words and phrases of the language in the area being visited.

- Beach bums – enjoy relaxing on a beach or around a hotel swimming pool. They relax by taking things easy and soaking up the sunshine, despite the health risks!

In reality, most people enjoy doing a variety of activities on holiday and it could be argued that there is a bit of the adrenaline junkie, beach bum and culture vulture in everybody. Part of the pleasure of planning a holiday is to take into account the wishes of everybody involved. The travel and tourism industry has to provide the products and services to meet all these needs, in the UK and overseas.

Enabling factors

Enabling factors are those which allow people to go on holiday. The two most fundamental are money and time. In the past, only rich people travelled extensively and went on holiday, and it is only in the last sixty years or so that most people in the UK have been able to afford a holiday. As residents of the UK have become wealthier, increasing numbers of people have been able to afford to take longer and more expensive holidays. The same thing is happening today in countries such as India and China with increasing numbers of people travelling internationally.

At the same time, people in the UK have more time to travel. Despite the pressures of modern living, the amount of paid holiday provided to many people has increased over recent years. This means that two or more tourism trips per year are now common. Related to this is the fact that life expectancy is increasing and people are living longer in retirement. This group of people have plenty of time and many have sufficient funds from their savings and pensions. Thus, this so-called 'grey market' is an important group of people for the travel and tourism industry to provide products and services for.

Another factor which has helped to increase the amount of tourism is that it is now much easier to travel to destinations. This can be considered in two ways.

1. Increasing car ownership

As more people own cars they are able to use their vehicles for a range of tourism purposes. These include:

● Driving to an airport before flying to a holiday destination;
● Using a car for a day visit to a seaside resort or countryside area;
● A touring holiday using a car, possibly in Europe, crossing the English Channel by car ferry;
● A camping or caravanning holiday using the car to tow a caravan or trailer tent;
● Travelling by car to visit friends and relations.

Many visits to countryside areas are made by car

2. Increasing transport provision

There has been a rapid development in transport infrastructure in recent years. This includes:

● Travelling from the UK to Europe using the Channel Tunnel by car or by train on Eurostar;
● The increasing availability of affordable air travel to more destinations than ever before.

Low-cost airlines have made air travel within Europe more accessible

- An expanding network of motorways throughout Europe making car and coach travel much easier;
- High-speed rail links throughout Europe;
- New bridges and tunnels;
- Many cities now have rapid transport systems;
- Modern transport is far more comfortable than it was in the past.

Modern coaches with air-conditioning and other features provide an alternative to car transport

Apart from having the time and money to travel and making use of modern transport infrastructure, there are other enabling factors to be considered. The marketing of tourism destinations is now more advanced so people are aware of the attractions and tourist facilities available in a city on the other side of the world.

Australia has marketed its attractions successfully in recent years

New technology, such as video, CDs and the internet, has made it possible to research destinations far easier than it was in the past. Additionally, it is now far easier to make travel bookings, either through a travel agent or from the comfort of your own home using a computer.

Exam preparation

1. Outline the factors which motivate people to travel.

2. Explain why the needs of business travellers are different from those travelling for leisure purposes.

3. Suggest why people are able to travel more today than they were in the past.

4. Evaluate the roles of different forms of transport in providing people with the opportunity to travel.

1.3 Defining tourism

From what has been covered so far it should be becoming clear to you that tourism is not an easy thing to define! So far a number of things have been discovered about the nature of tourism, including:

- Tourism is about far more than simply going on holiday – it includes business tourism and visiting friends and relatives as well;

- Tourism involves travel away from the area where a person usually lives;

- Tourism is essentially short-term – most tourist trips last less than one week, especially when business trips are included;

- Tourism is voluntary – with the exception of children who do not want to go on holiday with their parents, tourists make a positive choice about the places they wish to visit;

- Tourism is not only about staying away from home – although it is often the case that tourists are staying at least one night away from home, many people take day trips away from their normal place of residence, visit attractions and make use of other products of the travel and tourism industry.

Although there are many definitions of the term 'tourism', the following are used extensively in the industry.

The World Tourism Organisation, which is recognised as a leading body on global tourism, has developed the following definition:

'Tourism comprises the activities of persons travelling to and staying in places outside their usual environment for not more than one consecutive year for leisure, business and other purposes' (World Tourism Organisation 1993).

In the UK, the Tourism Society is a respected organisation representing a range of interests relating to tourism. The Society defined tourism as:

' Tourism is the temporary, short-term movement of people to destinations outside the places where they normally live and work, and activities during their stay at these destinations; it includes movement for all purposes, as well as day visits or excursions' (Tourism Society 1976).

Industry Info...

The World Tourism Organisation (WTO)

The WTO is an agency of the United Nations, acting as a global forum on tourism policy issues. The WTO encourages the development of responsible and sustainable tourism, paying particular attention to the interests of developing countries.

The WTO has a membership of over 150 countries and territories and more than 300 affiliate members representing private sector travel and tourism organisations, educational institutions and tourism authorities.

www.unwto.org

Industry Info...

The Tourism Society

The Tourism Society represents tourism professionals working in the United Kingdom. The society was established over thirty years ago to represent the views of people working in the industry as well as those working in universities and colleges. The Tourism Society also has student membership available.

The society is a member of the Tourism Alliance, which works to lobby both the United Kingdom and European governments about issues relating to tourism.

www.tourismsociety.org

It is not easy to count the number of day visitors coming into London to visit attractions such as the London Eye

Because of the problems involved in defining tourism, it becomes difficult to make precise calculations regarding a number of important questions, for example:

1. How many people take part in tourist activities? Although it is relatively easy to count the number of people passing through a port or airport, it is less easy to count those driving into the countryside or going to the coast for the day.

2. How much do people spend on tourism activities? Although it is possible to calculate how much people spend on travel and holidays, there are additional or secondary costs which should be considered. Before people travel on holiday they may need to buy sun creams, luggage and so on. Should these be counted as money spent on tourism? When people visit attractions it is common to identify the primary spend as the admission charge and secondary spend as money spent on food, drinks, souvenirs and other items while at the attraction.

3. How many people are employed in tourism? It is usual to identify direct and indirect jobs in tourism. Waiters in a hotel restaurant serving breakfasts to guests will be directly employed in tourism. However, the farmer who produced the eggs and bacon from the pigs he keeps is also earning money from tourism, as are other people employed in the food production process. The driver of a subway car in New York may be taking commuters into downtown Manhattan, but in the summer and autumn, a number of those travellers will be tourists. Is the driver part of the tourism industry?

Is a street entertainer part of the tourism industry?

Exam preparation

1. Why is it difficult to calculate the exact number of people taking part in tourist activities?

2. Explain the difference between primary and secondary spend on tourism products.

3. Explain why governments and other bodies want to find out how many people are employed in tourism.

4. Suggest why it is not easy to develop a definition of tourism.

The characteristics of travel and tourism

What you will study in this section

Introduction

In Section 1, we discovered that travel and tourism involves a great deal more than just going on holiday and in fact, on any one day, many people are travelling for business or leisure purposes into, out of or within the United Kingdom. These people are travelling to a variety of destinations which may be in European countries or anywhere in the world. At the same time, people from many countries are planning visits to, arriving in or departing from the United Kingdom.

The travel and tourism industry is responsible for providing products and services to allow all of these tourists' needs to be met. Travel and tourism companies and organisations provide transport for people travelling to destinations, accommodation for when they are away from home and attractions for them to visit and enjoy.

2.1 The travel and tourism industry

Travel and tourism is predominantly a private sector industry, made up of many commercial organisations that are in business to make a profit. They are supported by a variety of public and voluntary sector organisations that provide facilities and services for UK tourists and overseas visitors to this country.

Commercial organisations

The majority of the travel and tourism organisations providing products and services to travellers and tourists are commercial. This means they are aiming to make a profit from the goods and services they supply, whether it is a flight on an aircraft, a room for a night in a hotel or a visit to a theme park. All of these organisations must make sure that the money they receive from selling products and services is more than it costs them to provide the good or service. Otherwise, they will go out of business!

Hotels are privately-owned businesses aiming to make a profit by providing accommodation

Industry Info...

'bmibaby'

bmibaby is a relatively new low-cost airline set up as a subsidiary of British Midland Airways (bmi) in 2002. The airline is a good example of how commercial organisations must adapt to changing circumstances. Like other airlines, British Midland have established low-cost alternatives to compete with the big players in the market, such as easyJet and Ryanair.

bmibaby currently flies to over 50 destinations across Europe, with one of its main hubs, Birmingham International Airport, having routes to over 20 destinations. Like all low cost-carriers, bmibaby relies on its website for customers to make bookings.

www.bmibaby.com

Some of these organisations are large, global companies such as Virgin Atlantic, British Airways or Thomas Cook. Such companies have a turnover of millions of pounds and will be expected to make a profit for the shareholders who have invested in the company. However, the vast majority of travel and tourism organisations are small, independent enterprises such as small hotels, small attractions and independent travel agents. These are often referred to as small to medium-sized enterprises (SMEs). Such organisations operate very differently from large global companies, but their aim is the same – making a profit from selling products and services to tourists.

Industry Info...

Lynchpin Tours

Lynchpin is typical of thousands of small businesses which are the fabric of the travel and tourism industry. Lynchpin is run by two business men based in Portrush, Northern Ireland, who offer specialised tours for small groups of people visiting Ireland.

The company specialises in tailor-made tours which involve building the tours to meet the precise requirements of their clients. Specialised tours can be organised for golfers, honeymooners, and those interested in cuisine and genealogy. The main market for Lynchpin is American tourists who wish to play on Ireland's famous golf courses or discover more about their ancestors. Also, Lynchpin offers day tours to parts of Ireland for people taking cruise holidays which are visiting Irish ports.

Like many small to medium-sized enterprises, Lynchpin relies heavily on its website and on building personal relationships to attract new and repeat business.

www.lynchpintours.com

Non-commercial organisations

By no means all organisations providing products and services to tourists are run on a commercial basis. Non-commercial organisations, which may be publicly-funded bodies or voluntary organisations, also provide products and services to tourists. For example, most bodies providing tourist information are funded publicly. These include many tourist boards, such as VisitBritain, and local councils who run tourist information centres. These centres provide information to tourists about privately-run organisations in the area, such as hotels and attractions. So, very often, there is a relationship between commercial and non-commercial organisations working together to support tourists and meet their needs.

Industry Info...

VisitBritain

VisitBritain is the United Kingdom's National Tourist Office (NTO) which has the dual role of marketing Britain as a tourist destination to people from the rest of the world as well as promoting visits to England to people living in other regions of the United Kingdom.

VisitBritain is funded by the government through the Department for Culture, Media and Sport (DCMS) to promote Britain overseas as a tourist destination and to lead and co-ordinate England's tourism marketing.

www.VisitBritain.org

These relationships work in a number of ways. For example, a local council may be responsible for providing litter bins on a beach and for keeping the beach clean and safe. If a destination has a reputation for having a safe beach, more people are likely to visit and stay, creating more income and profit for commercial organisations providing accommodation.

Beaches are kept clean and tidy by publicly-funded bodies such as local councils

Other non-commercial organisations, known as voluntary organisations, also provide products for tourists. In the United Kingdom, the most well-known of these is the National Trust, which owns many areas of land used for tourism purposes as well as historic buildings that are open to the public. Visitors may pay to go into the properties, but the National Trust does not aim to make a profit, just to balance its income and its operating costs. Similarly, the Youth Hostels

Association aims to provide affordable accommodation, but does not aim to make a profit. Many small industrial attractions, such as railway centres, are managed by volunteers and do not aim to make a profit.

It is important to understand that, like in any other industry, travel and tourism organisations supply products to customers. A seat on an aircraft or a bed in

Industry Info...

The Foreign and Commonwealth Office (FCO)

The FCO is a department of the United Kingdom government which exists to work for the interests of United Kingdom citizens in a safe, just and prosperous world. The FCO has a network of more than 200 diplomatic offices spread all over the world. It is these offices which provide support to United Kingdom citizens when they need help while abroad.

The FCO also provides a range of advice to travellers before they travel, through a website which contains detailed, up-to-date information on known health and security risks to visitors in all countries which may be visited by United Kingdom tourists.

The FCO website is also used by the travel industry to obtain up-to-date advice which can be passed on to customers.

www.fco.gov.uk

The National Trust is a voluntary organisation and owns land used by walkers

The tour operator will calculate the cost of building and promoting the package holiday before adding on a profit margin to arrive at the selling price. Tour operators will attempt to maximise their profits by charging more when the holiday is likely to be more popular. This is why many travel and tourism products, such as flights and package holidays, are more expensive in peak periods such as school holidays and at Christmas.

Accommodation at hotels in resorts is a major component of a package holiday

a hotel room should be seen as examples of products of the travel and tourism industry. One of the most common products sold in travel and tourism is the package holiday. A package holiday is 'built' by a tour operator by buying seats on an aircraft and beds in a hotel, plus transfers (from airports to hotels) and possibly visits to attractions. The tour operator sells this product through a travel agent, or more commonly now, directly to the public.

Exam preparation

1. **Explain the main differences between commercial and non-commercial organisations in the travel and tourism industry.**

2. **What is meant by the term 'SME'? Give some examples of the products and services provided by five types of SMEs working within the travel and tourism industry.**

3. **Outline how a package holiday is a 'product' of the travel and tourism industry.**

4. **Evaluate the role and objectives of VisitBritain.**

2.2 External pressures on the travel and tourism industry

The travel and tourism industry operates in a constantly changing world and the industry itself has no control over many of the changes it faces. These are known as external pressures, as opposed to internal pressures which cause change within the industry. The move towards ticketless travel and online check-in are examples of internal pressures relating to changing technology.

External pressures on the travel and tourism industry can be grouped into two categories:

- Economic and political pressures;
- Environmental pressures.

Economic and political pressures

The travel and tourism industry is subject to a number of economic and political pressures over which it has no control. Quite simply, most people will not go on holiday if they cannot afford to and if a government puts a tax on a product such as aircraft fuel, or introduces some form of passport control, then the travel and tourism industry is affected in some way.

Economic and political pressures include:

- The economic climate – for most people, travelling is a luxury and people will go on holiday and travel for other purposes when they feel wealthier. Changes in economic conditions, such as employment rates, interest rates and other economic factors, will affect the amount of travel and holidays people can afford.

- Currency fluctuations – the values of world currencies are continually changing against each other. The most important of these changes is the value of the pound (sterling) against the value of the Euro and the American dollar. If the value of the pound is high against these currencies, it will be cheaper for people living in the United Kingdom to visit Europe or the USA. As the value of the pound falls, it becomes more expensive for United Kingdom residents to visit other countries, but cheaper for inbound tourists to visit the United Kingdom. In pricing products such as holidays to the USA, the travel and tourism industry must be aware of changes in the exchange rates between currencies.

- Fuel costs – a great deal of tourist activity is dependent on transport costs and these are very

A fly-drive holiday to the USA may seem less expensive when the pound is strong against the dollar and fuel prices in the USA are cheap.

Industry Info...

The weak American dollar

In the second half of 2007, the American dollar weakened against other currencies. For the first time, the exchange rate was over two American dollars to one pound sterling. The pound is now stronger against the dollar than it has been since 1992.

The impact of this is that more and more people are encouraged to visit the USA for a holiday because the cost of the holidays will be cheaper and goods and services will be less expensive as well. Those people visiting New York and other destinations on shopping trips will find lots of bargains.

Another impact is that other destinations, including Hong Kong, Cuba and many Caribbean countries, tie their currency to the US dollar. So if the dollar is weak, holidays to these destinations become cheaper as well.

Also, since oil and other fuels are sold internationally in dollars, they will also be relatively cheap, helping to make airfares slightly cheaper than they would be if the dollar was stronger.

Of course, it is impossible to predict for how long this situation will continue and what the impact would be if the dollar suddenly strengthened against the pound.

much affected by the price of oil. This in turn affects the price of aircraft fuel, petrol for cars and other fuel costs. Taxes are often imposed on fuel by governments to increase revenue. The travel and tourism industry has no control over the price of fuel, but must live with its consequences.

- Terrorist activity – the threat of terrorist activity has a range of impacts on the travel and tourism industry. These include:

- tourists are less inclined to want to travel to destinations where terrorist activity is likely;
- increased costs are incurred in safeguarding against terrorist activity;
- travellers are inconvenienced by having to pass through security checks and other security measures;
- the travel and tourism industry has to provide up-to-date advice and information to travellers relating to possible terrorist activity;
- governments may impose legislation relating to

Tourist arrivals to New York have now recovered to the level they were before the attack on the World Trade Centre in 2001

passport controls and requirements for visitors wishing to enter a country;

– tourists may choose to take more domestic as opposed to outbound holidays.

Environmental pressures

A great deal of tourist activity is related to the physical environment of the planet on which we live. Tourists enjoy visiting landscapes and environments they do not usually experience – warm temperatures, accompanied with light rainfall, are often appreciated by many UK tourists. Coastal areas with flat sandy beaches have become popular tourist destinations and major landscape features such as mountains, glaciers, waterfalls and canyons have become major tourist attractions.

However, society is becoming increasingly aware that the physical processes that are in operation on the surface of our planet can cause sudden catastrophic events while, at the same time, long-term climatic changes are taking place.

Environmental pressures can be related to landscape processes or climatic factors.

Landscape processes

These may have major impacts on the travel and tourism industry, as illustrated by the tsunami of 2004 in the Indian Ocean. The tsunami was caused by an underwater earthquake which created a tidal wave that hit coastal areas of India and Indonesia as well as other countries. Over 200,000 people are thought to have lost their lives. The travel and tourism industry in the area was severely affected at the time and tourism

Climate change, resulting in the melting of glaciers, is taking place in Arctic regions

infrastructure such as airports and hotels has had to be replaced in order to ensure that tourists continue to visit the countries affected at the time. There is no telling when a major earthquake, volcanic eruption, landslide or similar event might occur at a location popular with tourists. The travel and tourism industry must be prepared at all times to deal with emergency situations and have procedures in place for such events.

Climatic factors

There are many climatic conditions which cause external pressures on the travel and tourism industry. Perhaps the most significant events in recent years are the hurricanes which have affected parts of the Southern United States and Central Mexico.

On a smaller scale, the floods which occurred in the United Kingdom in the summer of 2007 affected the travel and tourism industry through cancelled bookings and disrupted holiday arrangements. In fact, the summer of 2007 was disappointing in a number of ways and many holidays were sold at the last minute as more people decided to leave the United Kingdom to escape the wet and cold conditions.

When weather conditions are different to what normally occurs, the travel and tourism industry is very often affected and, of course, the industry has no control whatsoever over the weather!

Winter sports resorts have become reliant on sufficient snowfall during the season when tourists book skiing holidays. In the Alps, this season normally extends from just before Christmas to mid-April. People living in these resorts are dependent on good snow conditions for their income and a resort's snow record will have an impact on its popularity.

Industry Info...

New Orleans hurricane

The city of New Orleans, in the southern state of Louisiana, was pummelled by hurricane Katrina in August 2005. The city was devastated and severe flooding occurred when the city's flood defences were breached. At one point 80% of the city was flooded, with some parts under 5 metres of water, and 90% of the residents had to be evacuated.

The city relied heavily on tourism, with 85,000 people employed in the industry in 2004. In that year, the city received over 10 million visitors spending over $5.5 billion in the city! In 2006, the city welcomed 3.7 million visitors spending $2.9 billion. Hurricane Katrina has had a dramatic impact on the tourism industry in the city as well as on United Kingdom-based tour operators and airlines.

However, the recovery has been remarkable, with a full programme of events planned to take place in the city during 2008.

www.neworleansonline.com

Ski resorts rely on sufficient snowfall to provide good conditions for skiing

Skiing is important for the economy of Alpine resorts

It may be that, over time, a period of warming will lead to a number of years when limited snowfall leads to poor skiing conditions or a shorter skiing season. To counteract this, some resorts in the Alps are developing other activities which will attract visitors at other times of the year so that the area is less dependent on winter sports for its tourism income.

It is not easy to predict the likely consequences of any long-term climate change on the travel and tourism industry in the future. Warmer winters may well lead to a reduction in the choice of winter sports destinations. Warmer summers might mean that more people are influenced to take their main holiday in the United Kingdom, if warm conditions can be guaranteed and, in certain Mediterranean areas, the climate may become too hot and uncomfortable in the summer months.

Industry Info...

Dateline: January 12th 2008

Two events reported in The Independent newspaper illustrate the external pressures over which the travel and tourism industry has no control.

'Snowfalls bring fresh hope to Scottish skiing industry'

This weekend there were perfect conditions for skiing at all five ski resorts in Scotland. All reported excellent fresh snow with virtually all of the ski runs open. This was very welcome news for the Scottish ski resorts which have had to battle their way through a succession of poor seasons because of warmer winters and low snowfall. Some of the resorts were able to open early because of the good conditions this year.

'Kenya's tourist industry counts the cost of unrest'

Elections held in Kenya in December 2007 led to widespread civil unrest and violence, including mass murders. Kenya has been seen as one of the most stable countries in Africa, with a well-developed tourist industry. At a time when the Kenyan tourist season should be at its peak, few tourists were coming to Kenya. The consequences of this are potentially devastating. About one million tourists visit Kenya each year making tourism Kenya's largest foreign exchange earner. About 500, 000 people are employed in the tourism industry and a further 500,000 are indirectly employed. Hotels in the capital city of Nairobi are operating on 10 percent of their capacity. United Kingdom-based travel companies, such as airlines and tour operators, will also be affected and those who have already booked may cancel their holidays.

www.magickenya.com

Source: Adapted from The Independent newspaper

Other external pressures

In recent years a number of events have had an impact on the travel and tourism industry in various ways. Examples of these include foot and mouth disease and bird flu. These events cause anxiety amongst tourists and discourage people from visiting the areas affected by the diseases. The foot and mouth outbreaks may have deterred visitors to the United Kingdom and bird flu made Turkey a less popular destination for a time.

When events such as these take place, the travel and tourism industry suffers through:

● A reduced demand for holidays to the area;

Some Mediterranean areas may become too uncomfortable for tourists during the hottest part of the year

- A reduced demand for flights to and from the affected area;

- Accommodation bookings are cancelled and the number of bookings decreases;

- Less people visit attractions;

- Non-tourism businesses in the area may have reduced travel requirements;

- Tourist boards have to work hard and undertake marketing campaigns to persuade tourists to start visiting the affected area again.

The travel and tourism industry has no control over any of the above factors – they are external influences. The industry must be able to adapt to changes in demand and on occasions, when there is a significant drop in demand for a certain product, some businesses may fail altogether.

Exam preparation

1. **Summarise the external pressures which the travel and tourism industry has to be prepared to respond to.**

2. **Outline how external pressures may cause travel and tourism businesses to fail.**

3. **Evaluate the possible effects on a 'strong pound' on inbound tourism to the United Kingdom.**

2.3 Technology in travel and tourism

There are many examples of the interactions between the development of technology and the evolution of the travel and tourism industry. However, these interactions can be divided simply into two categories:

1. Developments in transport technology
2. Developments in computer technology

Developments in transport technology

Developments in transport technology have allowed people to travel more quickly, safely and in greater comfort. Without the means to travel, people would find it very difficult to take part in tourist activities!

Land travel

There are two particularly significant developments in land-based transport technology which have allowed people to take part in tourist activities. These are the development of the railways and the development of the motor car.

The opening of the first rail services in 1825 allowed people to travel between major towns and cities in the UK much more easily. Steam trains and later railway technology allowed travel between and under cities, with underground railways being developed. Most of the development of the tourism industry in the latter half of the nineteenth century was due mostly to the spread of the railway system through the United

Kingdom, leading to the rise in popularity of seaside resorts such as Brighton, Margate and Scarborough.

It was the availability of rail services which enabled Thomas Cook to develop the first excursion in 1841. Cook's business grew rapidly in the middle years of the nineteenth century and he was soon developing a range of tours in the UK and Europe based on railway journeys.

Industry Info...

Eurostar

Eurostar is the name of the high-speed train linking London to France and Belgium through the Channel Tunnel. The service started in 1994 from Waterloo station in London, but since November 2007 the service has been operating from the newly-refurbished St Pancras station.

The fastest journey time on the London-Paris route is 2 hours and 15 minutes – city centre to city centre. Up to 17 Eurostar trains run from London to Paris each day and as many as 10 trains run to Brussels, with a journey time of 1 hour and 50 minutes.

A new station at Ebbsfleet International in Kent was also opened in November 2007, so that passengers can board Eurostar trains without travelling into central London. A similar facility operates at Ashford International station.

www.eurostar.com

In the early twentieth century, the advent of the motor car allowed people to travel with more freedom. After the Second World War, which ended in 1945, there was a massive increase in the growth of car ownership with more and more families being able to afford their own transport. This enabled them to visit other areas of the United Kingdom. Owning a motor car meant that tourists were not tied to railway timetables and had the independence to go wherever and whenever they wanted.

Additionally, technology has enabled the construction of bridges and tunnels above and below stretches of water to allow people to travel within the United Kingdom and to Europe more easily. The Severn Bridge linking England to Wales (opened in 1966) and the Channel Tunnel (opened in 1994) are examples of major feats of engineering technology which have facilitated easier travel by road and rail.

Car ownership gives more people access to countryside areas to take part in tourism activities

47

Air travel

There can be no doubt that the development of air travel during the twentieth century was a major influence on giving people the opportunity to travel. In particular, the development and introduction of the jet aircraft in the second half of the century made European and then long-haul destinations far more accessible to tourists from the United Kingdom. Technological developments allowed some aircraft to fly faster, such as the supersonic Concorde, or to fly with more passengers over longer periods. The Boeing 747 'jumbo jet', in particular, allowed United Kingdom tourists access to worldwide destinations and the new Airbus A380 jet, recently introduced by Singapore Airlines, carries even more passengers.

Modern jet aircraft provide long-haul flights to many destinations in a matter of hours

The technology of the modern jet aircraft allows people to travel at speeds of several hundreds of miles an hour at altitudes in excess of 35,000 feet above sea level. Today, major destinations such as the cities of New York and Washington on the eastern coast of the USA can be reached in about seven hours flying time. In comparison, steam ships took around 10 days to cross the Atlantic!

The former prison island of Alcatraz in San Francisco Bay is less than 12 hours flying time from the United Kingdom

Water-based transport

Stretches of water have formed barriers to travel in the past and ferries have been provided to allow travellers to cross rivers and seas. In the twentieth century, the development of the roll-on-roll-off ferry allowed for more efficient turn-round times, and on busy routes across the English Channel for example, the development of these ferries has allowed for faster journey times.

New fast ferries have cut the journey times on cross-Channel routes

For more than a century, tourists have combined the crossings of seas and oceans with the chance to relax on large ships. Although modern jet aircraft have reduced journey times, modern cruise liners have provided

The Canadian city of Vancouver is a popular port of call for cruise ships on the western coast of Canada and the USA

tourists with the opportunity to visit a number of destinations and cruise between them in relative luxury. Modern cruise ships are designed to be like floating hotels, with a range of entertainment facilities available on board. The great advantage of modern-day cruises is that tourists can fly to a destination before joining the cruise rather than starting at a United Kingdom port – this is known as a fly/cruise. Cruises to islands in the Caribbean Sea and Alaska are becoming increasingly popular.

Developments in computer technology

Developments in computer technology have revolutionised a number of aspects of travel and tourism, resulting in travel and tourism organisations having to go through a tremendous amount of change and giving rise to a range of new travel organisations.

As little as twenty years ago, all airline bookings were made by travel agents contacting airlines to make reservations. The airlines had used computers to develop computer reservation systems (CRS) to track and store the names of passengers booked on flights, departure times and other relevant information. Over time, CRSs of different airlines and other travel organisations became linked to form global distribution systems (GDS). These allowed travel agents to access information on flights directly, as well as being able to make bookings for car hire, accommodation and other travel services using computer technology.

The growth of the internet and home computers has had a very significant effect on the way tourism products are purchased. New companies, such as

Lastminute.com, Expedia, Travelocity and Opodo have been established to enable more people to book travel from the comfort of their own homes. These companies link internet users with the GDS networks of major travel companies, so increasingly travellers can book their flights, car hire and accommodation directly with the supplier rather than use the services of a travel agent.

Industry Info...

Opodo

Opodo is one of the major new online travel companies offering flights, car hire and hotel bookings through the internet. Opodo is owned by nine major European airlines and the Amadeus Global Distribution System (GDS). Opodo has access to:

- Flights from 500 airlines worldwide;
- Accommodation with over 600,000 hotels;
- 7,000 car hire locations worldwide;
- Travel insurance from AIG – the world's largest insurer.

The company also has the facility to offer online package holiday services, allowing customers to 'self-package' holidays.

Opodo was first launched in Germany in 2001 and its United Kingdom site has been in operation since January 2002.

www.opodo.com

In the same way, package holidays are now available online as well as through the high street travel agent. Brochures can be viewed on the internet, resorts and accommodation can be inspected using web-cams and prices can be compared.

Some travel organisations, in particular the major budget airlines such as Ryanair and easyJet, have encouraged the use of online travel by offering discounts for online bookings, thus avoiding the need to pay a commission to travel agents. The web sites of these airlines handle thousands of bookings per day, are continually being updated and can provide confirmation of a flight booking in seconds.

This change in booking air travel has been aided by technology which allows financial transactions to take place over the internet. Today, all major airlines allow the public to access their database of flight schedules and prices, and any traveller with a credit card can book a flight over the internet. 'Ticketless' travel means that a ticket is not issued and as long as the traveller has a booking reference, they have proof that they have a reservation and a printed ticket is not required.

Recent changes in technology have allowed for online check-in and self check-in at airports. Passengers can now choose their seat and print a boarding card before they even reach the airport. Some airlines allow a 'manage your booking' facility on their web sites, which allows passengers to choose and change their seat before they travel.

As well as allowing for major changes in the way that travel products are bought and sold, new technology is having other impacts on the way people travel. Immigration officials are using new technology to identify travellers in order to reduce the threat of terrorism. For instance, everyone entering the United States of America is obliged to have their photograph taken and their fingerprints recorded as they pass through immigration. This information is stored on a vast database to check for potential criminals and terrorists. At airports, scanning technology allows passengers to be checked for weapons and other devices, and CCTV allows the authorities to monitor people's movements in airports. Additionally, air traffic control systems allow the safe movement of aircraft through crowded air space and for aircraft to fly in weather conditions which would not have been safe a few years ago.

Exam preparation

1. **Outline the advantages and disadvantages computer technology has brought about for the travel and tourism industry.**

2. **Identify and explain how the jobs of people working in the travel and tourism industry have changed as a result of technological developments.**

3. **Assess the contribution the internet has made to providing information for tourists.**

Is the increasing use of technology all good news?

The increasing use of technology is raising a number of issues both within the travel and tourism industry and amongst travellers. These include:

- As people increasingly use the internet to book holidays and travel, are they receiving the same level of advice that they would from travel agents?
- Some civil liberties groups are concerned about the need to provide so much personal information to the authorities (such as providing passport details when booking flights to certain countries);
- There is an increasing threat of fraud and identity theft with so much personal information being provided by tourists;
- Concerns are being raised about the validity of information on sites which give reviews of hotels and resorts. Is this information genuine or have rival organisations posted the information?
- What happens if there are major faults in the system of an airline or credit card company, or the system used by air traffic control fails?
- Is the money paid to online travel companies protected in the same way as it would be through a bonded travel agency?

2.4 The products of the travel and tourism industry

The travel and tourism industry is like any other in that it provides a range of products and services which it promotes to potential customers in the hope of making a sale and making a profit from the sale. These products include holidays, flights and other forms of travel, hotel and other accommodation, car hire, visits to attractions, entertainment, etc. In addition, there are a range of products such as souvenirs, postcards and meals which are purchased during the course of a visit. Many other products are purchased in relation to travel and tourism ranging from cameras to sun creams and from clothing to insect protection.

The industry also provides a wide range of services. Each year, a variety of information guides are produced for different destinations, while tourist boards provide information centres to help visitors. Airlines offer a range of services provided by cabin crew during flights and other transport providers offer similar services.

However, there are a number of significant differences between the products of the travel and tourism industry and those provided by other industries, such as cars, TVs and furniture. This is because the main products of the industry – holidays – are about experiences.

The products of the travel and tourism industry are said to have a number of special qualities. They are said to be:

- Intangible;
- Perishable;
- Non-standardised.

Visiting a sun-drenched beach with clear blue skies overhead is what some people imagine to be the perfect holiday

Intangible

There are many examples of tangible products - a piece of fruit, a t-shirt or a computer are all tangible – they can be touched. Many of the products of the travel and tourism industry are intangible. In other words, they are experiences rather than something which can be physically touched or taken away as a lasting article.

This means that the product cannot be sampled before it is purchased. It is not feasible to sample a holiday before the holiday is booked or sample the first few minutes of a flight. For holidays in particular, brochures, promotional DVDs and websites play an important role in showing the potential customer what the holiday might be like. They are tools used to sell the holiday to the customer. Not all products of the travel and tourism industry are intangible – food purchased at a hotel or souvenirs bought at an attraction could be said to be tangible.

Perishable

This means that when the product has been experienced, it is over – it has literally perished. At the end of a holiday there is nothing to show but the experience; at the end of a flight the product has perished. You cannot take the seat with you!

The term perishable can also be applied to seats on a plane or hotel rooms. If a seat on a plane is not sold for a particular flight, that particular product has also perished. This is why last-minute holiday bookings can sometimes be bargains – the tour operator may as well try to get some money for the holiday as opposed to no money at all.

Non-standardised

Non-standardised refers to the fact that each tourist has a slightly different experience. If a family or group of friends travel together, each will have slightly different memories and the experience will not be quite the same for each individual. Every person may prefer one meal as opposed to another, one ride in a theme park as opposed to another, and so on. Therefore, the experience of tourism products is not the same for everyone – it is non-standardised. Also, two holidays taken in exactly the same accommodation and using the same airline, may well be totally different, given that different members of staff may be involved and the weather is unlikely to be exactly the same.

Section 3

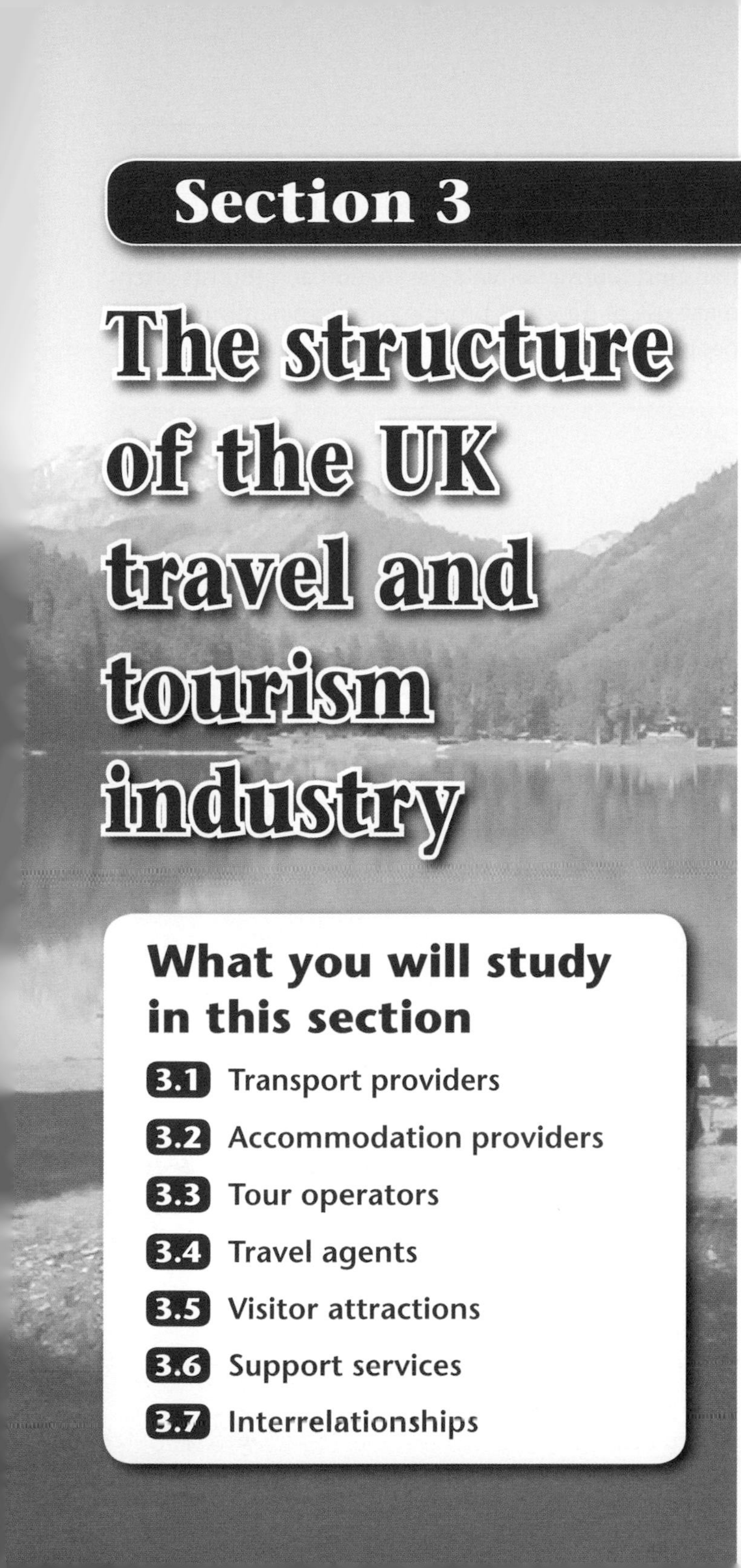

The structure of the UK travel and tourism industry

What you will study in this section

3.1 Transport providers

3.2 Accommodation providers

3.3 Tour operators

3.4 Travel agents

3.5 Visitor attractions

3.6 Support services

3.7 Interrelationships

Introduction

Organisations and businesses within the travel and tourism industry can be divided into the following six sectors.

1. Transport providers;
2. Accommodation providers;
3. Tour operators;
4. Travel agents;
5. Visitor attractions;
6. Support services.

As you will learn later in this section, organisations from different sectors must work together in order to provide products and facilities for tourists. For example, a day's coach outing to a theme park would involve two sectors working together, namely transport providers and visitor attractions. If the visit required an overnight stop, accommodation providers would be involved. This 'package' could be put together by a tour operator and sold through a travel agent. Whilst on the trip, people might visit a tourist information centre, which is part of the support services sector. This would mean that all six sectors are involved in the trip and organisations from each of the sectors would have to work together.

It is important to understand the difference between the six sectors of the travel and tourism industry and the three sectors of the economy – public, private and voluntary.

Some visitor attractions rely heavily on coach operators to bring visitors to the attraction

3.1 Transport providers

All tourism trips require different forms of transport to get people from their home to their destination. On many occasions, tourists may use a variety of forms of transport and for all holidays involving air travel, passengers must get to their departure airport by road or rail and then use transport from the arrival airport to their final destination. One of the advantages of using a private car for a holiday is that the car can take the holidaymaker from 'door to door' and there is usually more space for luggage.

There is no doubt that an effective transport network is essential for a successful travel and tourism industry. Tourists need to know that when they arrive at a destination, the transport they need to use is reliable and efficient. Tourists, whether travelling for leisure or business purposes, do not want to travel on overcrowded trains or get caught in traffic jams.

Once at the destination, tourists may make use of a variety of different forms of transport to get around. Taxis, trams, and underground systems are often used to transport tourists within a destination and tourists often make use of transport provided predominantly for local people.

Special tourist buses are used by many visitors to London, as they are in many cities

Organisations in the transport sector of the travel and tourism industry are often referred to as principals. These include:

- Coach operators;
- Car hire companies;
- Train operators;
- Ferry and cruise companies;
- Airlines;
- Airports.

Land travel

Land travel includes travel by road or rail – in the case of road travel, using private motor cars, coaches, taxis and hire cars.

Private motor cars

Cars offer more convenience and flexibility than any other form of transport. Everybody who owns a motor car has a great deal of choice over when and where they travel, and, for most domestic destinations, they can travel door to door. Many journeys involving international travel may begin with a car journey to an airport or railway station.

Cars are used most commonly for domestic holidays and day trips. However, many outbound UK tourists find taking a car to destinations in Europe, in particular France and northern Spain, to be convenient and affordable. In general, taking a car provides tourists with fewer restrictions on the amount of luggage that can be carried. This may be an important consideration for families with younger children.

Having the use of a car gives tourists access to far more places of interest

A surprising number of tourist trips in the United Kingdom are made by cars towing caravans. Caravans offer convenience and flexibility, with modern caravans providing a high degree of comfort. Caravan sites are available throughout the United Kingdom, northern Europe and further afield. In addition, camping is a popular type of holiday using road transport, with campers being able to carry tents and other equipment by car.

Many car journeys are made by business tourists, who need to travel to different destinations within the United Kingdom for business purposes. When these destinations are outside of the area where the person normally lives and works, the journeys are part of the travel and tourism industry. The regular daily journey to work by car (commuting) is not seen as part of the travel and tourism industry.

Coach travel

Coaches provide a number of services and choices for travellers. Firstly, coaches provide an alternative to rail transport between major cities. Companies such as National Express and Megabus offer a network of services between cities and large towns. These scheduled services are often cheaper than rail travel, but are sometimes slower and are subject to traffic congestion on motorways and city roads.

Scheduled coach services also provide links to airports from some major cities and railway stations in the UK, offering passengers an alternative method of travelling to their departure airport. For example, RailAir provides a coach service between Heathrow Airport and nearby major railway stations.

Industry Info...

Megabus

Megabus offers budget coach services between a number of major cities in England, Wales and Scotland, with prices for some journeys starting at just 50p plus a £1 booking fee. Many journeys are available for £5 or less and therefore offer a cheap alternative to rail transport.

The company uses internet technology in a similar way to the budget airlines, which allows passengers to view routes and schedules as well as making reservations online.

www.megabus.com

Coaches can be hired by groups of tourists who are going on a day's excursion or a touring holiday. Additionally, larger groups of tourists, such as school and college groups, may well find it convenient to hire a coach from the starting point of their journey to the airport they are departing from.

Coaches are also extensively used for touring holidays within the United Kingdom and Europe and there are a number of large commercial companies offering 'packaged' coach touring holidays with the cost of travel, accommodation and visits to attractions included in the price. One of the largest operators in the United Kingdom is Shearings Holidays. Coach holidays are favoured by older tourists and have the advantage of being relatively inexpensive as well as not requiring a member of the group to undertake the responsibilities of driving.

Shearings provide a wide range of coach touring holidays

Taxis provide an expensive alternative to public transport

Taxis

Taxis offer an alternative to scheduled public transport in cities and towns. Some tourists may prefer the comfort and reliability of getting to a specific destination within a city by using a taxi. This is especially the case if they are not confident using buses or an underground system, or if they are travelling late at night. However, taxis are always more expensive than public transport and tend to be used mainly for shorter journeys.

Car hire companies

These companies have offices in all major cities and in most airports. Hire cars can be used by tourists who are confident about driving in a different country and who wish to have the independence of visiting different places in their own time rather than travelling in groups on coaches. Major car hire companies include Avis,

Hertz, Budget, Europcar and Holiday Autos. Car hire companies can provide a range of vehicles to meet the needs of different travellers and provide one-way rentals so that the hirer can leave the car at a different location from where it was collected.

Travelling by train

Trains provide a range of travel options for tourists. Generally, trains run to a clear, published schedule and are an efficient way of travelling between city centres. Very often, travel by rail is a relatively cheap option if booked in advance, but rail travel can also be expensive at peak times. In many cases, high-speed trains make journey times between major cities in the UK much shorter than if completing the same journeys by road.

In the United Kingdom, rail travel is seen as relatively expensive and the level of service is often criticised.

Industry Info...

Hertz car hire

Hertz is the leading vehicle rental company in the world, operating from around 7,700 locations in 145 countries. Each year Hertz handles about 30 million rental reservations worldwide. The first car hire operation was in Chicago, USA in 1918 with just 10 cars and this company was sold to John Hertz five years later for $1 million.

Like all major car hire companies, Hertz has benefited from advances in technology. The company has utilised computer reservation technology since the 1970s and introduced an in-car navigation system called Never Lost in 1995 and satellite navigation systems are now available in most of its cars.

The car hire business is very competitive and, like other major car hirers, Hertz offers a range of loyalty schemes to encourage customers to use Hertz regularly rather than other companies. The most recent development occurred in 2006 when Hertz introduced a Green Collection of fuel-efficient, environmentally-friendly cars.

www.hertz.com

Modern coaches with air-conditioning and other features provide an alternative to car transport

Trains are run by train operating companies (TOCs), which run trains along lines owned and managed by a different company, Network Rail. This company also manages 17 key stations, but smaller stations are managed by the train operating companies themselves.

A significant addition to the rail network has been the introduction of the Eurostar service which runs from St Pancras Station in London to Paris and other major cities in Europe. Eurostar has significantly reduced the journey times between central London and Paris, and now provides an alternative to flying between the two cities. The high-speed track allows for the journey between London and Paris to be made in only two hours and fifteen minutes.

Additionally, underground rail systems, such as the London Underground and Newcastle Metro, provide transport options for tourists as well as residents of a city. Part of the appeal of some destinations to tourists is the opportunity to experience a city's underground system.

Comparing different forms of land travel

Tourists may have to make decisions between different forms of land transport for their journeys and a number of factors need to be taken into consideration. These include:

- The exact starting and finishing points of a journey – it may well be that the first stage of a journey is made by car to a railway station or airport although most of the journey is not made by car. Journeys starting from city centres are more likely to be made by rail;

- The composition of the group travelling – family groups with young children may well prefer the convenience of travelling by car;

- The cost of travel – many tourists are on a budget and cannot afford taxis, hire cars and other expensive forms of transport;

- The time of travel – it would not be convenient to catch a train if the journey needed to be taken early in the morning or late at night;

- The length of the journey – longer journeys are more comfortable by some forms of transport than others;

- The length of stay and what transport will be required while at the destination;

- The time of year and possible adverse weather conditions.

Exam preparation

1. Outline the advantages of taking a coach holiday for a couple or family group.

2. Assess the advantages and disadvantages of hiring a car while on holiday.

3. Evaluate the travel options for a group of business travellers travelling from Cardiff to Leeds for a three day conference.

Sea travel

Sea travel can be divided into two categories. Firstly, ferries are used when tourists need to cross a body of water to reach their destination. Secondly, cruise ships are used by people for whom the whole holiday is about travelling by sea, enjoying the facilities on board the ship and making excursions to attractions when the ship visits a port.

Ferries

There are a number of ferry routes operating around the coast of the British Isles. Many of these are vehicle ferries, which allow passengers to take their car or other vehicle on to the ferry with them. The most important routes operate between ports on the south coast of England and France, with the Dover to Calais route being the shortest and most popular. Other routes operate from Portsmouth, Poole and Plymouth.

The Dover to Calais crossing takes approximately one

hour and fifteen minutes, with two ferry companies competing for business on this route – P&O and SeaFrance. Until the opening of the Channel Tunnel, many tourists relied on cross-channel ferries to reach their destinations in France and other European countries. However, tourists now have a greater choice of travel options, since not only can they use the Channel Tunnel, but low-cost airlines have developed a network of routes to a number of cities in France. These developments have led to some cross-channel routes being discontinued.

Modern roll-on roll-off ferries are easier to load and reduce turn-around times in ports

Although the most important ferry routes for United Kingdom tourists are across the English Channel to Europe, it should not be forgotten that there are other ferries in operation. These include:

- Ferries from Liverpool and ports in Wales to the Irish Republic;
- Ferries to and from the Isle of Wight and the Channel Islands;
- Ferries from east coast ports to Scandinavia and northern Europe;
- Ferries between the mainland and the islands of Scotland.

The Fast Cat is a modern ferry linking Portsmouth with the Isle of Wight

Cruise ships

More and more United Kingdom tourists are choosing to go on a cruise holiday. Between 2005 and 2006 there was a 12% growth in the numbers, with approximately 1.2 million British people taking a cruise holiday. This is double the figure of 10 years ago. While the numbers taking package holidays as a whole remain static, the proportion taking cruise holidays continues to grow. The demand for cruise holidays is expected to continue to grow in the near future and cruise companies are building more, and bigger, ships to accommodate the growing numbers.

The Mediterranean area is the most popular destination, with many people taking the opportunity to fly from the United Kingdom to meet their ship at a Mediterranean

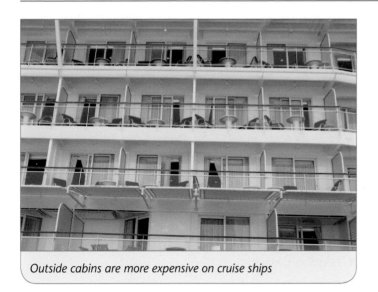

Outside cabins are more expensive on cruise ships

In recent years cruising has become fashionable and accessible, with more people being able to afford this type of holiday. In the past, cruising was seen as expensive and up-market with the need to dress for dinner. However, recently the cruise companies have provided a range of different options so that people can choose the type of programme which meets their particular needs. For example, some cruises cater for families and some for younger people. Another attraction of cruise holidays is that tourists are able to visit a number of destinations during one holiday while at the same time enjoying the facilities and comfort of a modern cruise liner.

Air travel

Air travel is the most popular method of travel for United Kingdom tourists making visits abroad and the

port. This is known as a fly/cruise. About 40% of cruise passengers start their journey at a British port, whereas 60% opt for a fly/cruise.

Industry Info...

The number of overseas visits made by United Kingdom residents has increased steadily.

United Kingdom residents' visits abroad from 1995 to 2005

	Visits by Air	Visits by Sea	Visits by the Channel Tunnel
1995	28,097,000	11,311,000	1,937,000
2000	41,392,000	9,646,000	5,799,000
2005	53,626,000	8,102,000	4,713,000

Adapted from International Passenger Survey data

importance of air travel in relation to other methods continues to grow.

In order to understand air travel in the United Kingdom it is first necessary to understand the relationship between airports and airlines. Both are commercial operations aiming to make a profit. Airlines make a profit through carrying passengers, whereas airports make a profit by charging airlines to land on the runways and make use of the airport facilities. These are known as landing charges. Airports also make money through charging retailers for space in departure lounges.

For example, at London Luton Airport the minimum charge for landing an aircraft is £138.77. The precise charge depends on the size of the aircraft, measured in tonnes. In addition, the airport makes a charge

Airports make money by charging retailers and food outlets for space in departure lounges

of £5.36 for each domestic passenger and £7.52 for each international passenger. There is also a security surcharge of £1 per passenger. Also, the airport charges airlines for parking their aircraft at the airport, depending on the amount of time the aircraft is on the ground (Source: London Luton Airport)

In the United Kingdom the major company operating airports is the British Airports Authority (BAA), which runs the following airports:

- London Heathrow;
- London Gatwick;
- London Stansted;
- Glasgow;
- Edinburgh;
- Aberdeen;
- Southampton.

Other major airports in the United Kingdom, including Manchester, Newcastle, Cardiff, Bristol and Birmingham, are owned by a variety of different organisations. London Heathrow is one of the world's busiest airports and, in comparison, the United Kingdom's other airports operate on a smaller scale. For example, Heathrow handles nearly 70 million passengers each year, whereas London Luton currently handles 9.4 million.

At Heathrow, the major airlines are the established full-service carriers such as British Airways, bmi and Virgin Atlantic. At Luton Airport the major users are the low-cost airlines, predominantly Ryanair and easyJet. At Heathrow, the most popular destinations include major cities, whereas at Luton domestic and short-haul destinations are more popular.

Industry Info...

Most popular destinations – 2006

Rank order	London Heathrow	London Luton
1	New York	Edinburgh
2	Dublin	Malaga
3	Paris	Glasgow
4	Amsterdam	Belfast
5	Frankfurt	Dublin
6	Los Angeles	Amsterdam
7	Hong Kong	Warsaw
8	Dubai	Geneva
9	Madrid	Paris
10	Toronto	Budapest

Source: BAA and London Luton Airport

All airlines operate commercially, aiming to make a profit by flying passengers (and sometimes freight) between destinations. As can be seen on page 63, the number of tourist trips from the United Kingdom has risen over the last ten years and air travel is now accessible to many people, whereas fifty years ago only rich tourists could afford to travel by air.

The differences between various types of airlines are becoming less clear as the nature of the airline industry changes. Traditionally, major airlines such as British Airways and Air France were known as 'flag carriers' and may have been publicly owned. Today, these airlines are owned by private sector organisations. Major airlines such as British Airways operate a scheduled service. This means that there is a published timetable which the airline follows for a set period of time. Aircraft fly on scheduled routes no matter how many passengers are carried.

Alternatively, aircraft may be chartered, usually to a tour operator which will lease the aircraft for a specific period of time to fly its package tour passengers to their chosen destinations. The operator is obliged to sell a high proportion of the seats on the aircraft in order to make it profitable.

In recent years, the distinction between scheduled and charter services has become less clear, with some tour operators, such as Thomson and Thomas Cook, operating their own fleets of aircraft.

One of the most significant developments in air travel over the last twenty years has been the emergence of low-cost or budget airlines. Of these, the largest operators are Ryanair and easyJet. The growth of Ryanair and easyJet over the last decade has been phenomenal. Their growth followed a change in policy by the European Union, which allowed new operators to compete with established airlines such as British Airways and Virgin Atlantic.

The table below shows the extent to which the number of passengers carried by Ryanair and easyJet has grown over the last decade. By comparison, Virgin Atlantic's growth has been more modest, but the airline is operating more long-haul routes and will make more profit from each of the passengers carried.

Industry Info...

Comparison in growth of passenger numbers between major airlines

Year	easyJet	Ryanair	Virgin Atlantic
1995	30,000	2,260,000	2,029,624
1996	420,000	2,950,000	2,293,802
1997	1,140,000	3,730,000	2,806,5538
1998	1,880,000	4,629,000	3,201,795
1999	3,670,000	5,358,000	3,622,402
2000	5,996,000	7,002,000	4,280,513
2001	7,664,000	9,355,000	4,105,115
2002	11,400,000	13,419,000	3,808,687
2003	20,300,000	19,490,000	3,850,578
2004	29,558,000	24,635,000	n/a
2005	32,953,000	30,946,000	n/a

Source: easyJet, Ryanair and Virgin Atlantic

Virgin Atlantic flies to long-haul destinations

How do low-cost airlines operate?

How does the operation of low-cost airlines differ from the established full-service airlines such as British Airways and Virgin Atlantic? As their name suggests, low-cost airlines do everything possible to reduce their costs and offer flights as cheaply as they can to passengers. This has been achieved by:

- Having a fleet of the same type of aircraft to reduce maintenance costs and allowing all pilots to fly the same aircraft.

- Flying to regional airports where landing charges are lower. Although this is often the case, low-cost airlines do fly to major airports as well, including Geneva, Barcelona and Paris Charles de Gaulle.

- Selling directly to the public as opposed to using travel agents which charge a commission on the sale of seats.

- Selling seats mainly through websites and originally through call centres. The websites are extremely sophisticated and are continually updated with the latest prices.

- Not providing passengers with free meals and drinks. In reality, these are never free, since on full-service airlines the cost of meals is incorporated into ticket prices.

- Asking cabin crew to clean aircraft between flights to reduce turn around times rather than using contracted cleaners.

- Offering very cheap or even free seats at off-peak times to attract customers. However, at peak times so called low-cost airlines will charge as much as the full-service carriers.

- Adopting a free seating policy rather than allocating specific seats to passengers. This saves administration costs and passengers are able to board their flight more quickly, again reducing the time the plane is on the ground.

- Having no business class seats so that any passenger can occupy any seat and some additional rows of seats can be added to the plane.

- Aggressive advertising that encourages passengers to take advantage of early bookings to obtain the cheapest prices.

- Flying on short-haul routes only, so that aircraft can make return trips to a number of destinations each day.

- Encouraging passengers not to carry excessive baggage. An additional charge is increasingly being made if passengers wish to check baggage into the hold of the aircraft. If the passenger has no hold luggage, the airline does not have to pay someone to load and unload it.

- Encouraging passengers to check-in online before they reach the airport so that the airline has to employ less staff, thereby reducing costs further.

The low-cost airlines have been so successful that they have forced the established full-service airlines to change their operational practices in order to compete. On popular short-haul routes to destinations such as Paris and Barcelona, the prices charged by traditional airlines may be similar to those of the low-cost carriers. On some short-haul routes free refreshments are now not served by full-service airlines. It is also now possible to book seats on British Airways and with other airlines using the internet.

Paris is now more accessible by Eurostar or by car either by cross-channel ferry or through the Channel Tunnel

There is no doubt that the emergence of the low-cost carriers has had a tremendous impact on air travel. Passengers now have far more choice on the type of air travel they use. Many passengers accept that free seating and no free refreshments are acceptable if they are flying to Barcelona or Madrid for a very low price with a budget airline.

Low-cost carriers have also had an impact on the operations of other travel and tourism organisations. More travellers are now able and prepared to book their flight directly with the carrier rather than using a travel agent. Furthermore, airlines have been responsible for 'self packaging', which is where the traveller books their own flights, accommodation and other transport, rather than buying a traditional package holiday. This is also known in the industry as 'dynamic packaging'. In addition, the number of passengers carried by cross-channel ferries has declined as more flights are available to destinations in Europe.

Exam preparation

1. Summarise the differences between a low-cost and full-service or traditional airline.

2. Outline the factors which business people need to consider when choosing whether to travel to Paris by Eurostar or by air.

3. Suggest why cruise holidays are becoming more popular.

4. Evaluate the impact made by the introduction of low-cost airlines on other travel and tourism organisations.

3.2 Accommodation providers

For many tourists, accommodation is a vital component of the travel experience. Apart from people visiting friends and relatives, all tourists require accommodation. People need to be comfortable and safe in their accommodation and feel that it is meeting their needs. Tourists have a wide range of accommodation types to choose from depending on the nature of the tourist trip they are undertaking, their budget and the composition of the party travelling. In terms of cost, rooms in the best hotels in major cities can cost up to £1,000 per night. At the other end of the scale, a bed in a hostel can cost only a few pounds. The majority of accommodation providers operate commercially – they are attempting to make a profit from providing accommodation for tourists. This applies to the

The Fairmont group of hotels owns the Chateau Frontenac hotel in Quebec, Canada as well as the Savoy Hotel in London

multinational hotel chains as well as a single farmhouse bed and breakfast establishment. The exception to the commercial nature of accommodation providers is the Youth Hostels Association, which operates as a charity, and some educational and religious organisations.

One of the principal ways of sub-dividing accommodation is into serviced and unserviced (or self-catering) accommodation.

Serviced accommodation

The essential ingredient of serviced accommodation is that the room in which the guest is staying is serviced in some way. This includes making beds, cleaning the room, changing the towels and stocking a mini-bar if one is present. Meals may also be provided by the establishment, but the essential ingredient of serviced accommodation is that the room is cleaned. It is not unusual for a hotel room to be occupied on a room-only basis – no meals are provided, but the accommodation is still serviced. Types of serviced accommodation include:

- Hotels;
- Motels and lodges;
- Bed and breakfast establishments;
- Guesthouses;
- Cabins on cruise ships.

Standard terms are used to describe the arrangements for serviced accommodation, such as:

- Room-only – the guest has only paid for the use of the room and is able to buy meals at an additional charge in the hotel restaurant or anywhere else;

- Bed and breakfast – the price charged for the accommodation includes the price of a room as well as a breakfast, normally taken in the hotel restaurant;

- Half-board - the price paid by the guest includes the cost of the room, breakfast and one meal. This is usually an evening meal taken in the hotel restaurant. The guest is expected to buy their lunch elsewhere;

- Full-board – the room and all meals are provided;

- All-inclusive – as well as all meals, the use of the hotel facilities, such as sports and fitness equipment, are included in the price. Usually, all-inclusive arrangements allow guests limited quantities of free alcoholic drinks as well.

Unserviced accommodation

With unserviced accommodation, the guest is responsible for making the beds and any cleaning. Very often, unserviced accommodation is also self-catering, but not always. For example, a complex of apartments may have unserviced accommodation, but there may be a restaurant available on site. Types of unserviced accommodation include:

- Cottages;
- Chalets;
- Villas and apartments;
- Camping and caravan sites;
- Second homes and timeshares;
- Canal boats;
- Home exchanges.

It is not possible to make a hard and fast rule in terms of serviced and unserviced accommodation. For example,

some apartments and chalets may be serviced, with the 'catered chalet' being a popular option for winter sports enthusiasts.

Self-contained holiday flats are likely to be unserviced

Types of accommodation

Different types of accommodation can be identified according to the range of facilities and services they have available for their guests.

Hotels

Hotels provide a wide range of facilities and services, which are open to guests or residents of the hotel as well as non-residents. Anybody can visit the bar or restaurant of most hotels for a drink or meal. Many hotels also provide conference and meeting facilities, and can cater for several hundred visitors as well as those staying at the hotel. Also, it is common for hotels to have leisure and fitness facilities, with swimming pools and saunas being common. Hotels may be part of an internationally-known chain, such as Holiday Inn or Hilton, or they may be family-run establishments with a small number of bedrooms.

Hotels in city centres are often expensive

Guesthouses

Guesthouses tend not to be open to the public in the same way as hotels. Restaurants and a bar, if provided, are for residents use only. Guesthouses tend to be small, family-run establishments with less than 10 bedrooms being common.

Bed and breakfast establishments

Very often, bed and breakfast rooms are provided within a private residence. Residents may or may not have the use of a lounge area, but no bar or restaurant will be available. Guests are not expected to stay in the establishment during the day, but leave as soon as breakfast has been served. Very often there will be 5 or less bedrooms in the establishment.

Lodges and motels

Lodges are a relatively recent development in the United Kingdom, which have developed from the American motel concept. Travelodge, Holiday Inn Express, Premier Travel Inn and Park Inn, are all examples of lodge accommodation. These establishments provide accommodation on a room-only basis, although a breakfast and meals in an adjacent restaurant may be available. They offer a standard bedroom, which is furnished to the same specification wherever the hotel is located. Lodges have the advantage of being located at convenient locations near motorway junctions and along major roads, thus being easily accessible for both business and leisure travellers. They can also be located at motorway service areas. The majority of guests using lodges are travelling by car.

The Travelodge chain provides accommodation on a room-only basis and guests can visit adjacent restaurants for meals

Industry Info...

Travelodge

Travelodge was the first lodge brand to be launched in the United Kingdom in 1985, over 20 years ago. Travelodge offer a standard double and family rooms in all of their lodges, situated at 240 locations throughout the United Kingdom. All rooms are en-suite, with king-sized beds, colour television and free tea and coffee making facilities. Rooms can be booked online, through a call centre or directly with the lodge itself.

Travelodges do not have their own restaurants, but are always situated next to a restaurant chain or fast-food outlet. They also do not have the range of facilities such as bars and lounges found in bigger hotels. A recent development is that the prices of rooms can be adjusted according to demand, with prices starting from £25 per room per night. A typical price is £59 per room per night. Travelodge accommodation is used by business and leisure travellers looking for reasonably-priced rooms for an overnight stay or to break a journey. The standard room found in all Travelodges is seen as an advantage, since customers know exactly what is on offer regardless of location.

www.travelodge.co.uk

Hostels

In the United Kingdom, most hostels are managed by the Youth Hostels Association (YHA), a voluntary organisation that aims to provide affordable accommodation for people while they are travelling. Most YHA hostels are situated in countryside areas and

Industry Info...

Youth Hostels Association (YHA)

The YHA operates over 200 youth hostels across England and Wales. The accommodation is open to anyone and everyone looking for affordable lodging, but the 230,000 members of the YHA receive a range of benefits including reduced rates for their stay.

The YHA operates as a charity with a mission to:

'Help all, especially young people of limited means, to a greater knowledge, love and care of the countryside, and appreciation of the cultural values of towns and cities, particularly by providing Youth Hostels or other accommodation for them in their travels, and thus promote their health, recreation and education'.

The YHA is always finding new ways to show that it offers a broad range of accommodation and services for different types of people in different localities. For example, from January 2008, the YHA has a licence to serve alcohol at over 150 of its hostels.

www.yha.org.uk

National Parks, encouraging people to enjoy the scenery and beauty of these areas. YHA hostels have different grades of accommodation, from simple to a more sophisticated level of comfort, plus accommodation specifically aimed at families.

Throughout the world, 'backpacker hostels' can be found in tourist areas, providing inexpensive accommodation for younger people travelling on a budget. Accommodation may only cost a few pounds a night, but guests may have to share rooms with strangers and prepare their own meals.

Young travellers will find backpacker hostels affordable and welcoming

Cottages, villas, gîtes and chalets

These types of accommodation provide self-catering holiday accommodation in a self-contained building. The building may have been constructed specifically for

tourist accommodation or may have been converted for tourist use in recent years. The accommodation is hired by the holidaymaker from the owner for a specific period, normally one or two weeks, but longer periods are not uncommon.

This type of accommodation appeals to larger family groups or friends who are happy to 'do their own thing' rather than have to conform to the requirements of a hotel. The holidaymakers need to be prepared to do all of the usual household tasks and in the majority of cases, will need private transport to reach attractions and other facilities.

A relatively recent innovation in the United Kingdom has been the introduction of the holiday village. This purpose-built accommodation is situated in quiet country areas. The villages are self-contained and

In many alpine areas, traditional chalets have been converted into tourist accommodation

holidaymakers are provided with a range of leisure activities and facilities. The most well-known of these developments are the four Center Parcs holiday villages in England. Holiday villages have evolved from the holiday camps developed by Billy Butlin and Fred Pontin in the mid-twentieth century.

Camping and caravan sites

Most people spend at least one night of their lives sleeping in a tent. Camping remains a popular activity, with several thousand camp sites in the United Kingdom. The Camping and Caravan Club has over 1,200 listed sites alone. Camp sites offer a range of facilities from basic toilet blocks to modern facilities with bars and restaurants on sites. Some camp sites have swimming pools and offer activities as well. Camping is also a popular option for United Kingdom residents who enjoy driving to the French coast and other areas to stay on camp sites.

Additionally, there are thought to be over one million caravan owners in the United Kingdom. Modern caravans are very well equipped and usually have

Camp sites can provide additional income for farmers

shower and toilet facilities as well as a fridge and oven. Caravan owners enjoy the freedom of being able to move from site to site and the comforts of their own 'home from home'. The majority of camping and caravan sites are run as private enterprises, with a significant number run by farmers for whom the site produces significant income during the summer season.

Second homes

Increasing numbers of United Kingdom residents are now able to afford to buy a second home. Until 20 years ago, second homes were mainly purchased by more affluent people living in urban areas of the country who wanted a home in the country as well. Areas of south west England in particular, as well as parts of Wales, have suffered from property prices being inflated because of the demand for second homes. This meant that young people living in the area were unable to afford to buy their own home. More recently, parts of western France, coastal areas of Spain and north Italy have become popular with United Kingdom residents buying second homes. Very often, the property is old and may need renovating, but increasingly villas and apartments are being built specifically to be sold as second homes. This is especially the case in Spain, where there is sometimes an oversupply in certain areas.

A number of areas of eastern Europe are now being explored as destinations where second homes can be purchased cheaply. This is particularly the case in Croatia and Bulgaria. In many destinations, property companies are being established to provide estate agency services to United Kingdom residents looking to purchase a second home.

Second home ownership abroad has become more

Coastal areas of Croatia are experiencing rapid development, with apartments being built and sold as second homes

or two specific weeks that they have purchased. They have the use of the apartment and facilities for those specific weeks only. However, with most timeshare arrangements, the owner can exchange their weeks for time in another property at another destination. This is seen as one of the great advantages of timeshare ownership. One of the largest organisations providing timeshares is Resort Condominiums International (RCI).

popular because people are increasingly able to buy houses at prices cheaper than property in the United Kingdom. Very often people buy property in an area they have visited on holiday in the past, perhaps on a number of occasions. Many second homes are bought as a long-term investment, perhaps as a retirement home for those people who have retired in their fifties and can travel easily to and from their second home. The affordability of flights has also assisted the growth of second homes in Europe, with areas close to the destinations served by low-cost carriers often experiencing a rise in property prices.

Timeshare

The timeshare concept involves a company building accommodation with a range of facilities and selling 'time slices' of the property to clients. Thus, a person may buy an apartment within the property for the one

Industry Info...

RCI – Resort Condominiums International

RCI acts as an exchange agency for people who own timeshares so that they can exchange the weeks they own for space in other resorts. RCI has over 3 million members worldwide and exchanges timeshare properties in some 3,700 locations.

Timeshare owners typically pay between £6,000 to £8,000 to own one week in a resort property. The cost of the timeshare will depend on the location and what time of the year the week is bought. RCI's role is to act as an agent offering the owners the ability to exchange their property weeks for a holiday in another location. RCI will also arrange flights.

www.rci.com

Purpose-built resorts, such as Whistler in Canada, have a significant number of timeshare developments

Accommodation grading schemes

Accommodation grading schemes are used to provide tourists with information about the quality of the accommodation they are booking or intending to use. They are developed by tourist boards and other bodies to provide tourists with information about the quality and range of facilities and the standard of the accommodation on offer. Traditionally, hotels have been awarded stars, based on the quality and range of services they provide, with the highest available rating being five stars. Tourists associate a five-star hotel with comfort, luxury and quality, and would expect to pay a premium for these attributes.

As well as hotels, budget hotels, lodges, self-catering accommodation and campsites are also given a star rating, depending on the level of services provided.

Although the rating system provides some indication of the nature of the accommodation, such systems are not without their problems. Because the criteria assess the range of services rather than the quality, tourists cannot necessarily guarantee the quality of the accommodation. In the past, tourist boards and motoring organisations, such as the Automobile Association (AA), have used different criteria, which has caused confusion. Since 2006, VisitBritain, VisitScotland and the AA have designed common standards across all accommodation grading systems. In addition, tour operators have used their own accommodation grading systems to give people booking holidays some indication of the standard of accommodation being provided. These schemes vary between different tour operators.

Accommodation providers may have to display information relating to different grading schemes, which may confuse potential customers

> ## Exam preparation
>
> 1. **Compare the advantages of staying in serviced as opposed to unserviced accommodation.**
>
> 2. **Explain why it is important for tourist destinations to provide a range of accommodation for visitors.**
>
> 3. **Evaluate the range of accommodation provided in one named destination you have studied.**

3.3 Tour operators

Tour operators have traditionally been the 'builders' of holidays. Quite simply, the tour operator buys the components of a holiday – flights, accommodation and transfers – and puts them together as a package. So, a typical package holiday, such as two weeks at a Mediterranean resort with full-board and transfers, would consist of a flight, accommodation, meals and airport transfers. Because these components can be bought in bulk, the tour operator can usually provide the holiday cheaper than if the customer bought and arranged each component of the holiday separately.

The tour operator is often referred to as a wholesaler of holidays, selling products through a retailer, who is the travel agent. The suppliers of transport, accommodation and other components of the holiday are referred to as principals.

Industry Info...

Example of a price breakdown for a package holiday.

Flight	£125
Accommodation	£195
Transfers	£20
Tour operator's profit	£35
Travel agent's commission	£20
Total cost to the customer	**£395**

Package holidays are attractive to some tourists because so much of the organisation is done for them

As the UK tourism industry developed through the second half of the twentieth century, tour operators became successful in providing an ever-increasing range of package holidays to leisure tourists. They were able to produce brochures showing destinations and accommodation options, with prices for the holidays shown. Customers would go to their high-street travel agent to collect brochures from different operators featuring the holiday area they wanted to visit. When a choice had been made, the tourist returned to the travel agent to make a booking. The travel agent would receive a payment from the tour operator, called a commission, in return for making the booking and recommending the holiday.

Although this relationship between travel agents and tour operators still exists today, a great deal has changed in the last ten years as more and more tourists are able to contact both the tour operators and principals directly using the internet. At the same time, the major holiday companies have changed the way they operate and are able to sell more of their holidays directly to the public without using travel agents. Some tour operators have become travel agents as well.

Types of tour operator

Within the United Kingdom, there are some 600 organisations working as tour operators. These can be grouped into one of the following categories:

1. Mass-market tour operators;
2. Specialist tour operators;
3. Domestic tour operators;
4. In bound tour operators.

Mass-market tour operators

These operators specialise in selling high volumes of holidays, mainly to traditional short-haul coastal destinations. However, in recent years, more package holidays to long-haul destinations have been sold through mass-market operators. These companies include some of the most familiar names in the travel industry including Thomson (TUI), MyTravel, Thomas Cook and First Choice Holidays.

These so-called 'big four' provided holidays and flights for nearly 12 million people in 2005. However, the companies have been finding it increasingly difficult to sell package holidays as more people find it more convenient to make independent arrangements through making use of the internet. In the second half of 2007, mergers between Thomas Cook and MyTravel, and Thomson with First Choice Holidays, took place. From now on, the 'big two' – TUI UK/Thomson and Thomas Cook – will be better placed to compete with other travel organisations.

Mass-market tour operators may employ 'reps', who are based in larger hotels in popular resorts to provide support to their customers

Specialist operators

As their name suggests, specialist tour operators specialise in particular types of holidays, rather than providing mass-market products. Very often a specialist tour operator will provide holidays to a specific country or offer adventure tours to a region such as the Amazon or South East Asia. The company will be able to provide in-depth knowledge about the area in which they operate, unlike the mass-market operators. These specialist companies are becoming more popular as customers look for a more individual type of experience rather than a mass-market product.

Domestic tour operators

Domestic tour operators provide package holidays which take place within the United Kingdom. One of the leading providers is WA Shearings (a merger between two coach holiday companies, Wallace Arnold

Domestic tour operators generally use less expensive accommodation in order to make the tours more affordable to their market

and Shearings). This type of holiday is more favoured by older holidaymakers who enjoy the companionship of the coach journeys to regions of the United Kingdom they may not have visited before.

Inbound tour operators

It should be remembered that in global terms, the United Kingdom is an important tourism market. Many people living in countries throughout the world hope to be able to visit the United Kingdom at some point in their life. Each day, travel agents in different countries sell package tour holidays to the United Kingdom. Independent travellers also book flights and accommodation to allow them to visit this country. A large number of these tours are based on the heritage, gardens and castles found throughout the United Kingdom, while London remains one of the prime destinations for inbound holidaymakers from around the world. There are over 200 inbound tour operators providing a range of holiday options for overseas visitors coming to the United Kingdom.

3.4 Travel agents

The role of travel agents is to sell holidays and other travel products to the public. There are nearly 6,000 travel agents in the United Kingdom which are members of the Association of British Travel Agents (ABTA). Most of these are leisure travel agents, selling holidays and short breaks. Business travel agents are more specialised and meet the needs of companies and business travellers.

Retail travel agencies

Retail travel agencies are either independently owned or part of a chain of agencies owned by the same company – these are called multiples. Chains such as Thomas Cook and Thomson operate several hundreds of shops each.

Independent travel agents are single businesses which are not part of a chain and are often managed by an owner or small team of staff. Independent travel agencies are free to offer their clients a wide choice of holidays provided by a number of operators. These travel agents trade on their ability to provide their clients with a very personal service and rely very much on their reputation within the locality in which they operate.

The multiple travel agencies are in fact owned by tour operators and sell the holidays produced by the major tour operators. This relatively recent change is known as vertical integration. In the past, it was more common for travel agencies to offer the holidays provided by a number of tour operators, and independent travel agents still do. However, if the travel agency is in fact owned by a tour operator, it may favour selling the holidays provided by that operator.

Traditionally, the travel agents' role was to advise the customer about which holiday was most suitable for them. However, independent travel agents are finding it increasingly difficult to compete against the larger organisations. Retail travel agents sell a wide range of travel products. As well as holidays and flights, the travel agents sell travel insurance, car hire, coach and rail travel as well as theatre tickets and currency exchange.

Selling cruise holidays is one area of growth for leisure travel agents

Many travel agents benefit from a high-street location

Over the last decade, many travel agents have found business difficult. Most of the products they sell from high-street stores are now available on the internet, often at cheaper prices. More travellers can buy travel products from the comfort of their own home. However, the larger multiple travel agents are still seen on the high streets of most towns. This is for a variety of reasons, including:

- The name of the company is visible, so that potential customers remember the name when they are thinking of booking a holiday;

- The travel agency may attract passing trade as people walk along the high street;

- Being on the high street promotes a successful image and gives potential customers confidence in the company;

- People working in businesses situated on the high street will have the opportunity to visit the travel agency going to and from work and during their lunch hour.

Business travel agents

Business travel involves travelling for meetings, attending conferences, taking part in trade fairs and exhibitions. It also includes 'incentive travel', where travel opportunities are provided for workers as prizes for meeting targets or for other work-related achievements. Business travel agencies offer specialised services, such as dealing with high-spending clients who have specific needs, or providing complex itineraries at short notice. Very often, business travel provides a high return for travel agents when they are providing services for major organisations. However, as in other areas, today's business travellers are able to make their own arrangements online. By no means all business travel is undertaken by highly-paid executives!

Call centres and home workers

Call centres are used by companies in a number of fields to provide customers with an alternative way of booking holidays and purchasing other travel products. They have grown with the introduction of Teletext and television travel channels. Clients are able to dial a number and discuss their travel requirements with a counsellor over the telephone. Once a holiday has been arranged, payment can be made by credit card. Call centres have been found to be an efficient way for travel companies to operate without the costs associated with having a high-street presence. Within the travel and tourism industry, call centres are used by tour operators, travel agencies, car hire companies, airlines and tourist boards.

Technological developments mean that travel agents do not need to be located in an office to carry out their business. Home workers, with access to a computer terminal with internet connections, can access all of the information they require to sell holidays and make bookings. A number of companies, such as Travel Counsellors, have a network of home workers who can be contacted in their homes to make travel bookings for customers.

Online travel agents

Increased availability of internet facilities has led to a rapid rise in the number of travel products sold by 'virtual travel agents'. These companies, including lastminute.com, Expedia and Travelocity, have vast databases linked to airline and accommodation providers, which can offer information on prices and schedules within seconds. These companies benefit from speed and flexibility, although the client is less likely to receive the impartial advice they would from a high-street travel agent. Additionally, increased onus is placed on the customer to make the correct booking. If the customer makes a mistake in the booking of flights or accommodation, they may not be able to reclaim their money in the same way as they would if they had made their booking through a travel agent. Nevertheless, online travel agents have seen tremendous growth in recent years and are likely to be the way in which most travel products are sold in the future.

3.5 Visitor attractions

Tourists are unlikely to visit any destination if it has very few attractions. Attractions literally 'attract' tourists to an area. Tourist destinations with a wide range of attractions are more likely to be successful because they can attract different types of tourists to visit different types of attraction! There are a number of ways in which attractions can be classified. It is common to distinguish between natural and purpose-built attractions. In addition, buildings and other sites that were not built as visitor attractions have become popular places to visit over time. These include castles, cathedrals and heritage sites such as Stonehenge. In recent years, heritage attractions, such as the Jorvik Viking Centre in York, have been developed and industrial sites, such as Ironbridge in Shropshire, have been turned into living museums. Additionally, facilities such as sports stadiums are seen as attractions – even when they are not being used for matches and major sporting events they are seen as attractions as they offer tours to visitors.

Tours of the Millennium Stadium are a popular attraction for visitors to Cardiff

Natural attractions

Throughout time, travellers have always been interested in discovering new landscapes and gazing at magnificent natural features. Looking at dramatic natural scenery is part of the basic appeal of travelling. Modern-day travellers can reach destinations which, a hundred years ago, were virtually inaccessible.

Within the British Isles, there is a rich variety of landscapes – from dramatic coastal scenery to highlands, moors, forests and mountains. As people began to travel further from their homes, they became amazed at the variety of landscapes and features that could be found around the British Isles.

One of the reasons why so many overseas visitors are

Bryce Canyon National Park in Utah, USA, contains spectacular landforms created by the action of wind and water on soft rocks

In many cases, different organisations have provided facilities for visitors close to natural attractions. Important attractions, such as those in National Parks, may have visitor centres with car parks, toilet facilities, refreshment facilities and interpretation centres with education facilities. Very often, footpaths are provided to allow access for enjoyment of the natural surroundings. The great majority of natural attractions are free to visit, but some, such as cave systems, are on private land and an entrance fee is charged.

Because there are so many, it is not easy to list the most significant natural attractions within the United Kingdom. The table on page 86 contains some of the most well-known examples.

Ladies View above Killarney in south west Ireland became famous over 100 years ago after ladies in waiting travelling with Queen Victoria visited the area and looked down on a landscape of mountains and lakes

attracted to the United Kingdom and the Irish Republic is the beautiful coastal scenery, rugged mountains, peaceful lakes and picturesque valleys. As well as being 'attractive' in their own right, many natural attractions provide opportunities for tourist activities. Tourists might enjoy walking and climbing on mountains to get excellent views and enjoy the mountain air; canoeing and kayaking can be undertaken along rivers and a range of water sports take place on lakes. Many upland areas provide opportunities for rock climbing and abseiling. Surfing is increasingly popular in many coastal areas and a sandy beach on a hot afternoon has always been appealing to tourists wishing to relax and unwind or to swim in the sea.

Stanage Edge in the Peak District is a popular climbing location

Speedwell Cavern is one of a number of cave systems near the village of Castleton in the Peak District National Park

It is important to appreciate the difference between individual natural attractions and tourist areas within which there will be a number of attractions. For example, Snowdonia, the Pennines and the Lake District are all mountain areas in which there would be a number of individual attractions, some of which would be natural and others purpose-built. Also, it is difficult to calculate the number of visitors to natural attractions. Whereas in many purpose-built attractions visitors enter through a gate or door, perhaps paying an entrance fee, it is far more difficult to calculate the number of visitors to a natural attraction, unless an entrance fee is paid,

Industry Info...

Examples of natural attractions in the United Kingdom

Type of attraction	Examples
Coastal features	• The Giant's Causeway in Antrim, Northern Ireland • Beachy Head in Sussex • Golden Cap on the 'Jurassic' coast of west Dorset • Oxwich Bay beach on the Gower coast of south Wales
Mountains	• Ben Nevis in Scotland • Mount Snowdon in north Wales • The Cuillin Hills on the Isle of Skye • Hellvelyn in the English Lake District
Lakes	• Lakes Windermere and Wastwater in the Lake District National Park • Lake Bala in mid Wales • Lough Neagh in Northern Ireland
Caves	• Dan-yr-ogof caves in south Wales • Wookey Hole in Somerset • Blue John Cavern in Derbyshire
Waterfalls	• Aberdulais in south Wales • High Force in North Yorkshire • Gaping Gill in Yorkshire

Niagara Falls in Canada

such as to visit a cave. Many of the natural attractions in the United Kingdom are found within the National Parks. These areas were set up in the mid-twentieth century to protect some of the most spectacular landscapes in the country and to provide opportunities for people to enjoy the areas and take part in leisure activities.

Many outbound tourists from the United Kingdom choose to visit destinations that have world-famous natural attractions. These include Niagara Falls in Canada, Bondi Beach in Australia and The Grand Canyon in Arizona, USA. Despite the rich diversity of the natural landscapes in the United Kingdom, a range of landscape features, such as canyons, geysers, glaciers and volcanoes, are not found in the country. Therefore, tourists have to visit other regions of the world in order to see these natural attractions.

The Grand Canyon in Arizona is a major natural attraction which is visited by millions of tourists each year, including outbound tourists from the United Kingdom

Purpose-built attractions

Purpose-built attractions are exactly that! They are places and buildings designed to attract people to visit them for leisure and other purposes. Most purpose-built attractions are run on a commercial basis, although some may be operated as charities. An organisation constructs an attraction in the expectation that, over time, sufficient numbers of people will spend money visiting the attraction so that the organisation makes a profit.

There are a number of ways to classify purpose-built visitor attractions. One method is to identify:

- Leisure attractions;
- Parks and gardens;
- Heritage and cultural attractions;
- Events.

Leisure attractions

The largest leisure attractions are theme parks and amusement parks. These are amongst the most visited attractions in the United Kingdom with well-known brand names such as Alton Towers, Thorpe Park, Blackpool Pleasure Beach, Oakwood and Drayton Manor

Park being amongst the most popular. Theme parks are all about excitement and enjoyment with extreme rides and lots to do. They offer a full day of activities and rides, attracting thousands of visitors, mainly throughout the summer months.

The British weather makes it uneconomic and impractical for most theme parks to be open all year round. Recently, more parks have been taking the opportunity to open until mid-November in order to provide Halloween-based events and experiences for their visitors. Generally, theme parks have a number of 'blockbuster' rides which are the primary attraction for many visitors. However, theme parks contain a variety of facilities that appeal to a wide range of customer types.

Blackpool Pleasure Beach is not a beach!

Major theme parks in the United Kingdom receive millions of visitors each year – Blackpool Pleasure Beach is estimated to have received over 6 million people in 2005. Several others receive over 2 million visitors annually. These figures indicate the scale of operation

of major theme parks. Entrance fees to these attractions average about £20 per person, suggesting that the turnover may be as much as £50 million per year. New rides may cost several millions of pounds to develop. Therefore, it is understandable that very few new theme parks are being opened. The last major theme park opened in the United Kingdom was Legoland, Windsor.

As with natural attractions, United Kingdom outbound tourists are attracted to overseas destinations that have major theme parks. Since the 1980s it has become increasingly popular to travel to the Disney parks in Florida and California. Also, Disneyland Paris is now an attractive alternative. However, the park does suffer from its location, being rather cold in the winter months.

Port Aventura in Spain is open virtually all year round, partly because the climate is so much warmer than it is in the United Kingdom

Some popular holiday destinations in Europe have theme parks located close to them. An example is Port Aventura in Spain, which is situated just outside the resort of Salou, about an hour south of Barcelona.

Parks and gardens

Although parks and gardens do not attract the same volume of visitors as theme parks, they are significant in that they are found throughout the United Kingdom and are open all year round. Kew Gardens in West London has been attracting visitors for a very long time – long before any theme park was open in the country. The Eden Project in Cornwall is a new concept in terms of being a purpose-built attraction as well as being an important ecological and environmental project.

Zoos can also be included in this category. Again, these have been important purpose-built attractions for a

Parks and gardens are found throughout the United Kingdom – their visitor profile is different to that of theme parks

number of years, with London Zoo, Chester Zoo and Bristol Zoo being amongst the most popular. A novel development has been the opening of safari parks, such as at Longleat in Wiltshire.

Industry Info...

Longleat

Longleat comprises a number of attractions on one site. The Safari Park was the first of its type opened outside Africa in April 1966. Animals roam freely across enclosures covering 250 acres (100 hectares) and seven miles of road winds through the park. There are over 400 animals living in the park. Longleat has benefited in recent years from the filming of the BBC series Animal Park, following the working lives of the rangers and the animals they look after.

Longleat House is an historic property owned by Lord Bath. Tours of the house are available and there are rooms available for conferences and events. In the grounds of Longleat House are a range of attractions including:

- Postman Pat Village
- Rides on safari boats
- Adventure castle
- Longleat railway
- Motion simulators
- Tea cup ride

www.longleat.com

Heritage and cultural attractions

There are many heritage and cultural attractions situated throughout the United Kingdom, which are popular with inbound and domestic tourists. These places are important not merely as visitor attractions, but to help preserve the culture and heritage of the country.

- Historic properties – castles and palaces are found throughout the country and some of these have a history spanning many hundreds of years. Windsor Castle attracts thousands of visitors each year, attracted by the chance to visit the Queen's residence. Likewise, Buckingham Palace in London is open at certain times of the year. Some castles and palaces are still occupied, while others are ruins, but still attract visitors because of their historic significance.

- Churches and cathedrals – all major places of worship attract significant numbers of visitors annually. Canterbury and Winchester cathedrals are important to the tourist economy of both cities. Tintern Abbey in the Wye Valley is just one example of a ruined church that attracts visitors to its very scenic location.

- Museums and galleries – major art galleries and museums attract many thousands of visitors annually. In fact, the British Museum in London has some 4.5 million visits per year. Tourists are attracted by the opportunity to see certain exhibits or the chance to study a famous painting.

- Military museums – there are a significant number of sites where visitors are attracted by the military history of the United Kingdom. These include the RAF Museum at Duxford in Cambridgeshire and the Historic Dockyard in Portsmouth. In the same town is the D-Day Museum, dedicated to the events of the Normandy landings in the Second World War.

HMS Victory, Lord Nelson's flagship at the battle of Trafalgar, is still officially a serving ship of the Royal Navy as well as being a visitor attraction

- Industrial museums – as the industrial landscape of the United Kingdom changed during the second half of the twentieth century, some of the most important industrial sites have been transformed into museums. This was in order to preserve the skills and culture of the people who lived and worked in those times. Major industrial museums include Beamish in County Durham, the Black Country Museum in the West Midlands, Ironbridge Gorge Museum in Shropshire and Big Pit in South Wales. These are sometimes referred to as 'living museums' because visitors can watch live demonstrations of traditional crafts or listen to actors pretending to be people who would have lived at the time in which the museum is set.

At the National Slate Museum at Llanberis in North Wales, workers cottages are preserved as they would have been furnished when they were inhabited

Qatar, in the Middle East, hosted the Asian Games in 2006 and is now bidding to host the Olympic Games in 2016

It is important to appreciate that many heritage and cultural attractions did not start off being tourist attractions. They were built for a very different purpose and have become tourist attractions over time. These are sometimes referred to as secondary tourist attractions, because tourism was not their main function. Those attractions that were built specifically for tourism are primary attractions.

Events

Events attract tourists to an area as well as providing for the needs of local people who attend the event. Events occur on a number of scales, with the biggest, including the Olympic Games and Football World Cup, played every four years after a long period of preparation. For

such events, new facilities (purpose-built) and sports stadiums are constructed.

Other sporting events, which occur on an annual basis, draw in thousands of people and make a significant contribution to the local economy. Examples are the Wimbledon Tennis Championships and the British motor racing Grand Prix at Silverstone. Events need not be related to sport. Music festivals, such as Glastonbury and the Reading festivals, attract many rock music lovers each year, while the Edinburgh Festival attracts tens of thousands of people to the city each August. Another example is the Notting Hill Carnival, which is a celebration of Caribbean culture. It takes place every year in west London during late summer.

Small to medium scale events are held all over the United Kingdom throughout the year. They provide tourists with a reason to visit a particular place and help support the local economy.

In recent years more events have been organised around the Halloween period

Visitor numbers to attractions

Obtaining precise information about the numbers of visitors to different attractions can be difficult for several reasons. For many natural attractions there is no specific entrance. For example there may be several paths by which people can climb a mountain and they don't have to pay, so no figures are kept.

Government policy has resulted in many major attractions, such as museums and galleries, not charging for entry. Therefore there may be no formal way of counting visitors. This will be especially true in the case of smaller museums. In paid attractions, which operate commercially, the owners may be reluctant to publish precise information about the exact number of visitors received for commercial reasons.

Nevertheless, it is important to attempt to obtain some idea of how many people are visiting different attractions and what trends are taking place over time.

VisitBritain publishes information about visitor numbers to major attractions annually. The following information is taken from a press release relating to the *2006 Survey of Visits to Attractions in England*.

- 196.5 million visits were made to attractions in 2006, a +3% increase over 2005 with the average adult price to visit an attraction being £5.21.

- Attractions in urban areas increased by +6% compared to coastal areas (+1%) and rural areas (-1%).

- Visits increased to most types of attraction: in 2006, 86.9 million visits were made to gardens, 54.6 visits were made to museums and galleries and 47.1 million visits were made to historic properties.

- The ten most popular paid attractions were:
  1. The Tower of London (2.1 million visits)
  2. St Paul's Cathedral
  3. Great Yarmouth Pleasure Beach
  4. Flamingo Land Theme Park, North Yorkshire
  5. Metroland, Gateshead
  6. Windermere Lake Cruises
  7. Kew Gardens
  8. Chester Zoo
  9. The Eden Project
  10. Canterbury Cathedral

- The ten most popular free attractions were:
  1. Blackpool Pleasure Beach (5.7 million visits)
  2. The Tate Modern
  3. The British Museum
  4. National Gallery
  5. Natural History Museum
  6. River Lee Country Park
  7. Xscape Castleford
  8. Science Museum
  9. Victoria and Albert Museum
  10. National Portrait Gallery

Museums and galleries in London attract millions of domestic and inbound visitors each year

3.6 Support services

The term 'support services' is usually applied to the tourist boards and other bodies that support the other sectors of the travel and tourism industry. Generally, these are non-commercial organisations set up by governments to support the work of the tourism industry. Many governments recognise the importance of tourism to the economy and have set up national tourist boards to co-ordinate efforts to promote their country to potential inbound tourists.

In the United Kingdom, as in many other countries, public sector involvement operates at three levels:

- National level – through the work of government departments, National Tourist Boards and government agencies;
- Regional level – activities undertaken by Regional Development Agencies and Regional Tourist Boards;
- Local level – through local authorities.

The principal government department responsible for tourism policy is the Department for Culture, Media and Sport (DCMS). The department sets the agenda for tourism and supports the industry by providing funding and helping to promote a positive image of the United Kingdom internationally.

Other government departments that have an indirect involvement in tourism include the Department for Transport and the Department for Environment, Food and Rural Affairs (DEFRA). One outcome of the outbreaks of foot and mouth and other diseases has been the realisation of the value of tourism to the rural economy in Britain.

National Tourist Boards

The UK has four National Tourist Boards:

- VisitBritain – this organisation is responsible for promoting the whole of Britain as a tourist destination to potential inbound visitors. It does this by providing information to individuals, and more importantly through working with travel and tourism organisations in other countries in helping them to arrange visits to Britain. VisitBritain also promotes England to visitors from other parts of the United Kingdom;
- Visit Wales – aims to develop the tourism product in Wales through effective marketing, while at the same time improving economic and social prosperity;

- Visit Scotland – exists to support the development of the tourism industry in Scotland and to market Scotland as a quality destination;
- Northern Ireland Tourist Board – responsible for the development, promotion and marketing of Northern Ireland as a tourist destination.

The national boards are funded mainly from central government sources, channelled through the DCMS, Welsh Assembly Government, Scottish Executive and Northern Ireland Assembly.

Regional Tourist Boards

Regional Tourist Boards (RTBs) work closely with the Regional Development Agencies (RDAs). The RDAs are funded from central government to promote economic development, including tourism, in their areas. The RDAs and RTBs work in partnership to develop future plans for tourism development and marketing. There are currently nine RTBs in England and four Regional Tourism Partnerships in Wales.

Local authorities and tourism

Many local councils in cities, as well as county and district councils, recognise the value of tourism in terms of creating jobs and bringing income into the local economy. Local authorities may support tourism in a number of ways, including:

- Providing promotional leaflets, brochures and websites;
- Maintaining parks and gardens;
- Maintaining local theatres and arts centres;
- Providing an accommodation booking service.

Tourist information centres (TICs)

Tourist information centres is the generic term most commonly used for offices and other places where tourists go for information about the destination they are visiting. In fact, there are a number of differences in the services provided by different TICs, depending on the nature of the organisation which is funding them. TICs may be funded by Regional Tourist Boards, local authorities, National Parks and sometimes other organisations. The service they offer will depend to a certain extent on where they are located as well as the organisation through which they are funded. All TICs provide information about local attractions and accommodation. Many offer a range of local produce for sale, as well as maps, guidebooks and souvenirs.

National Park Information centres provide visitor information about activities taking place within the park

Tourist guiding services

Tourist guides are also normally included in the support services sector of the travel and tourism industry. Guides are extremely useful in providing tourists with key information about the destination they are visiting. In some attractions, the only way to visit is by taking part in a guided tour – visitors are not allowed to wander by themselves.

One of the principal tourist guiding bodies is the Blue Badge Guide scheme. This UK scheme represents qualified people who have been trained to provide guided tours of cities and other destinations. They have a wealth of knowledge about the destination and help the tourist to enjoy a more informative visit. Blue Badge Guides are contracted on a daily basis by tour operators to provide guided tours.

Tourist guides provide information to make visits more interesting

3.7 Interrelationships

Very seldom do tourists buy a product from the travel and tourism industry which does not involve the co-operation of organisations working in different sectors of the industry. This can be demonstrated through the case of a standard package holiday:

- The holidaymaker buys the package from a travel agent;

- The holiday has been put together by a tour operator before it was sold by the travel agent;

- The tour operator would have arranged flights and transfers from the airport by working with transport providers. Transport providers may well have transported the holidaymaker from their home to the departure airport;

- The tour operator will also have worked with accommodation providers in order to provide the holidaymaker with somewhere to stay;

- During their stay, the holidaymaker may well make visits to attractions;

- The holidaymaker may also visit a tourist information centre to find out information about attractions in the area, making use of a variety of support services.

The above example demonstrates one way in which organisations from different sectors of the industry are interrelated. In many destinations, these relationships are supported by the local authority and tourist board, which may provide a forum in which the different organisations can come together to discuss issues.

Package holidaymakers make use of the services of organisations working in all sectors of the industry

Quite often, the local tourist board and council work hard to support the commercial organisations that are bringing tourists to the destination. The local council may well be involved in cleaning the beaches, providing transport for tourists, providing information centres, supplying beach facilities and more.

Showers are provided close to the beach in Salou

Section 4

The development of the UK travel and tourism industry

What you will study in this section

Introduction

People have always travelled for a variety of reasons. However, the concept of holidays being taken in exotic locations by ordinary people is a fairly recent development. At the time of the Roman Empire, two thousand years ago, citizens of Rome would spend the summer in villas along the coast to escape from the heat of the city. Merchants and traders have always travelled between cities looking for articles to buy and sell, while throughout history people have travelled for religious purposes. Explorers such as Christopher Columbus, Sir Francis Drake and Marco Polo were travellers, discovering new lands and then returning to their home ports to tell stories about places that nobody else had visited.

However, until 200 years ago, the vast majority of ordinary people never travelled far from their homes in their entire life. They did not have the opportunity or the means to travel – transport between cities was restricted to horses, carts and stagecoaches, and it was extremely slow and sometimes dangerous.

In the United Kingdom it was the development of the railways that first gave people the means to travel longer distances away from their homes. At about the same time, through the nineteenth century, more affluent people were beginning to travel to the seaside to enjoy the fresh sea air. Bathing in the sea also became popular since it was believed that it was healthy to do so. Thus, the foundations of the United Kingdom travel and

Many of the tourist facilities in Blackpool, including the North Pier, were built during a short period in the mid-nineteenth century

tourism industry were laid in the middle years of the nineteenth century as the railways opened up access to seaside resorts. Famous seaside towns such as Brighton, Bournemouth, Scarborough and Blackpool grew at a rapid rate as more facilities were provided for tourists.

Concurrently, more people were working in factories in the great industrial cities and some of these people could afford the occasional day visit to the seaside – travel and tourism was no longer only available to the wealthy elite.

During the early years of the twentieth century, more and more ordinary people were beginning to be able to travel to the major seaside resorts. Very often, railways provided the means of travel, however people also travelled to seaside resorts just for the day on coaches

Industry Info...

The resort of Blackpool illustrates the rapid development of the major seaside towns during the nineteenth century:

- 1846 – first railway line constructed to Blackpool;
- 1852 – gas lights were installed;
- 1856-70 – a promenade was constructed;
- 1863 – the North Pier was opened;
- 1868 – the Central Pier was opened;
- 1878 – the Winter Gardens were opened;
- 1885 – an electric tramway was opened;
- 1894 – Blackpool Tower was opened.

The Winter Gardens has provided entertainment for visitors to Blackpool since 1878

4.1 Holiday camps

To cater for those who could not afford to stay in hotels and guesthouses, holiday camps were established in the early years of the twentieth century. Holiday camps were composed of wooden chalet accommodation buildings and also offered meals and entertainment. The first holiday camps were, in some cases literally, campsites with tents for accommodation. Holiday camps established in the 1920s boasted 'brick chalets with running water, electric light and modern toilet facilities'.

Campers were encouraged to take part in group activities and evening entertainment was provided. For people used to working long hours in factories, without television or radios at home, this was seen as a luxury. By the 1930s, holiday camps were established as an alternative to hotels and guesthouses. Some of these were run by trade unions, which provided holiday facilities for their members. Many others were operated commercially. However, in the middle years of the 1930s, an entrepreneur who had made money from fairground amusements opened the first of his properties near the resort of Skegness on the Yorkshire coast, and the holiday camp concept was taken to a whole new level!

Billy Butlin is seen as one of the pioneers of the United Kingdom tourism industry. He did not invent the holiday camp, as is commonly believed, but developed much bigger and better camps compared to those which had existed previously. The Butlin's holiday camp at Skegness opened in 1936, offering high-class interior features, plus a wide variety of entertainment and attractions, and was larger and more impressive than any of its rivals. In fact, Billy Butlin was so successful

called charabancs. It was normal for people to travel with families or work colleagues who would be given the same day or week off work by factory owners. Often, all the factories closed for the same week and everybody went to the same resort for a week's holiday.

Despite economic problems and the coming of the First World War (1914-1918), the pattern of tourism to seaside towns became part of the British way of life. Nevertheless, it was during the 1930s that things began to change rapidly. Up until that time, there were still many people who were not able to enjoy an annual holiday. They may well have been unemployed, had poorly paid jobs or were not entitled to annual holidays. However, for those who could afford some form of holiday, entrepreneurs began to offer an alternative to hotel accommodation – this was the concept of the holiday camp.

because he had no direct competition. His camps were bigger and better than those offered by his competitors.

The Butlin's product offered a 'week's holiday for a week's pay' and targeted working-class families with one-price, pre-paid holidays. The services provided by the holiday camps included individual chalets for families, shops, hairdressing services, floodlit swimming pools, childcare services, ballroom dancing, tennis, bowling and boating. To a certain extent, the Butlin's concept was targeted at the 'struggling housewife' who, without the aid of modern labour-saving devices, was seen as working hard to bring up a family. Butlin's offered these people the chance to experience something they had not had the opportunity to do so before.

A second Butlin's holiday camp was opened at Clacton in Essex in 1938 and a third was being built at Filey, not far from Skegness. It has to be remembered that many visitors to Butlin's holiday camps had never been on holiday before. Their parents' generation very often had not been on holiday and so the relative comfort and range of entertainment was much appreciated by the 'campers'. The needs and expectations of Butlin's clients were far less sophisticated than those of today's tourists. People were happy to eat set meals at set times and enjoyed the entertainment which was not available in their own homes. Also, campers were happy to be looked after by the staff of the camps called 'Redcoats', named after the colour of their uniforms. These people could be regarded as the first generation of 'reps' or resort representatives that helped to organise visitors during the day and provided their entertainment in the evening.

It is important to appreciate that the 1930s was a period of rapid social change. The First World War had ended some years earlier and many people had lost fathers, brothers and husbands. People wanted to move on with their lives and try to take advantage of the greater leisure time which was available to them. Also, in the late 1930s, it was increasingly likely that there was going to be another war with Germany, so people were taking the opportunity to enjoy themselves while they could. In fact, when the Second World War started in 1939, the Butlin's camps were taken over as military bases. At this time camps were under construction at Ayr on the west coast of Scotland and Pwllheli in north Wales.

Industry Info...

Butlins

The development of the Butlins network of holiday camps and other properties grew rapidly in the post-war period;

- 1945 – holiday camp at Filey opened;
- 1946 – camps at Skegness and Clacton re-opened;
- 1947 – camps at Ayr and Pwllheli opened;
- 1948 – Billy Butlin began to open hotels at locations across the UK and in the Bahamas;
- 1960s – further holiday camps opened in Bognor Regis, Minehead and Barry.

www.butlins.com

There is no doubt that the Butlin's holiday camp concept captured the mood of the nation at that time and was extremely successful at meeting the needs and expectations of people who were not used to travelling and going on holiday. Another factor in the success of the Butlin's holiday camp business, and other similar products offered by Pontin's and Warner's, was the introduction of the Holidays with Pay Act in 1938. Working conditions in the factories and mines of the Industrial Revolution had been gradually improving during the latter half of the nineteenth century and the early years of the twentieth century. Acts of Parliament were passed relating to child labour, factory conditions and so forth. The passing of the Holidays with Pay Act marked the end of a twenty-year campaign for paid holiday time for workers. The Act introduced the entitlement of one week's annual paid holiday for all full-time workers (remember, today most full-time workers receive three or four weeks paid holiday per year).

Holidays With Pay Act 1938

1938 c.70 1_and_2_Geo_6

An Act to enable wage regulating authorities to make provision for holidays and holiday remuneration for workers whose wages they regulate, and to enable the Minister of Labour to assist voluntary schemes for securing holidays with pay for workers in any industry.

[29th July 1938]

The Holidays with Pay Act represented a milestone in British social history. It provided ordinary working-class people with the opportunity to take part in leisure and tourism activities in a way they had not been able to before. The Act created a whole new market of people with the desire and means to take part in tourism activities. Holiday camps were developed specifically to meet the needs of this new market, who could now participate in tourism activities which, hitherto, had only been available to the middle classes. As such, it created the first generation of mass tourists.

Holiday camps were only one way in which patterns of leisure and tourism were changing in the years between the two World Wars. By the early years of the twentieth century, there was a growing appreciation of the 'great outdoors'. People had begun to appreciate the splendour and beauty of the highland areas of Britain and had an increased desire to visit them. The benefits and pleasure of outdoor recreational activities, such as walking and cycling were being appreciated by more people. At the beginning of the twentieth century there was growing conflict between landowners and interest groups such as the YHA, the Council for the Protection of Rural England and the Ramblers' Association regarding access to the countryside.

Other developments

By the early 1930s, the government was looking into the establishment of National Parks in the United Kingdom, but no direct action was taken. In response to this, mass trespasses were organised by pressure groups on Kinder Scout in Derbyshire, demanding access to countryside areas. In 1936, the same year as Billy Butlin opened his first holiday camp, the government began the process of looking into the establishment of the first National Parks in the United Kingdom. Again, the onset of the Second World War delayed the process, but following the end of the war in 1945 the government introduced the legislation which set up the National Parks. The first National Park in the United Kingdom was the Peak District, having been established in 1951. By the end of the decade, ten national parks in total had been designated.

The Peak District was the first area to be designated a National Park in the United Kingdom in 1951

So, the 1930s and 1940s represented a period of social change in which ordinary working-class people were increasingly able to take part in leisure and tourism activities. They were entitled to paid holiday periods for the first time. Holiday camps provided an opportunity to experience a real holiday and there was an increasing desire to visit and appreciate the most scenic areas of the country.

By the end of the 1940s, more and more workers were being given longer periods of paid holidays and the

numbers of hours worked each week were steadily declining. By 1951, two-thirds of all workers had two weeks paid holiday rather than just one. Thus, there was an increase in the amount of time many people had to take part in leisure and tourism activities. Along with the increase in leisure time which many people now had, was increased mobility through the use of motor cars. Before the Second World War, only wealthy people could afford motor cars, in the same way as only wealthy people were able to afford to travel in the previous century. As more households were able to afford to purchase a motor car, increasing numbers of people could visit the countryside or seaside whenever they wanted, rather than having to rely on public transport.

In 1950, it is estimated that there were approximately 2 million cars in the United Kingdom. By 1970, this had increased to around 11 million. In 1951, about 14% of households had the use of a motor car; by the year 2000, this had increased to 73%. This increased mobility led to a number of changes in terms of where people lived in relation to where they worked or shopped. It was increasingly possible to drive to places in an hour or so, which would have taken much longer without the use of a motor car.

People enjoyed the freedom to go where they wanted and when they wanted. They could go into the countryside or visit a seaside resort for a day or a short holiday and did not have to rely so much on public transport. By the end of he 1950s, a new development had taken place. The first section of motorway was opened in 1959 and there were near 400 miles of motorway by the mid-1960s. One impact of this was that tourist destinations further away from the main towns and cities became more accessible. Holiday areas in Cornwall and Scotland became far more popular as people became more confident in driving longer distances to their holiday destinations. As increasing affluence provided more families with the opportunity to buy a motor car, another technological development provided people with a new type of entertainment and means of receiving information – this was the television.

Television ownership increased dramatically during the 1950s; by the end of the decade the majority of households in the United Kingdom had access to a television, whereas in 1950 very few people owned one. Television programmes gave people information and insights into other countries in a way that pictures and magazine articles never could. This fuelled people's desire to travel. They were able to travel throughout the United Kingdom in their motor cars – now they were ready to venture further a field!

4.2 Mass tourism and package holidays

In the last section we saw how changing socio-economic conditions (holidays with pay) and technological developments (the motor car and railways) led to large numbers of people being able to take a holiday and visit the countryside and seaside resorts in the United Kingdom. This could be argued to be mass tourism, since large numbers of people were travelling to the same destination for a holiday. However, the term 'mass tourism' is more usually used to summarise the development of inbound tourism to Mediterranean countries from the 1960s onwards.

While increasing car ownership led to increased domestic tourism through the 1950s, another development in transport technology was also beginning to become significant. This was the development of the jet aircraft. Aircraft technology had advanced considerably during the Second World War. When the war ended in 1945, these developments could be put towards commercial use. In the 1950s, there were further significant developments in the design of jet aircraft, which were able to fly faster and for longer periods of time, as well as carrying more passengers. During the 1950s, the first commercial jet airline passenger services had commenced and the first passenger airline service to Australia took off in 1959.

Industry Info...

Boeing 707

The Boeing 707 is seen as the aircraft which really opened up the skies to short-haul and long-haul passenger travel.

The aircraft began operating in 1958. It could carry up to 180 passengers, had a range of 3,000 miles and could fly at 600 miles per hour. Its arrival marked the beginning of modern air travel.

www.boeing.com

The 1950s also saw the very first package holiday using air travel. Vladimir Raitz of Horizon Holidays organised a tour to the Mediterranean island of Corsica in 1949. The aircraft used had 32 seats and the full-board accommodation was in tents, but nonetheless the modern package holiday had arrived! In the first year of operation, some 300 passengers were carried. These humble beginnings laid the foundation of the present-day package holiday business, which developed through the second half of the twentieth century. The growth of package holidays is synonymous with the development of what is understood as mass tourism.

Mass tourism, as the term suggests, involves large numbers of tourists all travelling to the same destination. However, it is important to consider the concept of mass tourism a little more closely:

- Mass tourism destinations are generally located on coasts, with most visitors looking for a 'sun, sea and sand' holiday;

- Most mass tourism destinations developed as centres for package holidays, with a significant number of visitors arriving on chartered aircraft and staying in pre-booked hotel accommodation;

- Holidays to mass tourism destinations are predominantly organised by private-sector travel organisations, with relatively few visitors travelling independently;

Many Mediterranean coastal resorts have become associated with mass tourism

- Many mass tourism destinations have a distinct high season in the summer months. Different client groups might occupy the accommodation at different times of the year.

Therefore, resorts on the Spanish Costas, such as Benidorm, Alicante and Marbella, would be seen as mass tourism destinations. Large cities, such as Paris, Rome and New York, although they receive large number of visitors each year, would not be classed as mass tourism destinations.

The developments in aircraft technology and the coming of the jet aircraft in the years following the Second World War, made destinations around the Mediterranean coast far more accessible from the 1950s onwards. At the same time, increased affluence in the United Kingdom and other European countries made it possible for more people to consider a package holiday to a Mediterranean destination. Another factor in the development of mass tourism to Mediterranean coastal areas was the governments of Spain and other countries welcoming the influx of visitors. Planning regulations were relatively lax and it was easy to build high-rise tourist accommodation close to the beach. In addition, there was a ready supply of labour, with people moving in to coastal resorts from the poorer rural areas inland. Although a number of long-term disadvantages resulted from this process, at the time tourism was seen as a boom industry in Spain and many individuals and organisations were keen to take advantage of the opportunities available.

Throughout the 1960s and 1970s, increasing numbers of tourists from the United Kingdom chose to take package holidays to Spanish mass tourism resorts as well as to resorts in other European countries, such as Greece

Industry Info...

Inbound tourism to Spain

There has been a dramatic increase in the number of tourists visiting Spain in the last 50 years and the country remains second only to France in the list of countries with the most international visitors.

- In 1950 there were less than 1 million international tourists to Spain;
- By 1960 this had increased to 6.1 million;
- In 1970 there were 24.1 million tourists;
- By 1980 this number had grown to 38.1 million;
- In 2007 there were over 50 million international tourists.

Most of Spain's international tourists come from other European countries including France, Germany and the United Kingdom.

Recent studies have indicated a reduction in the number of 'sun, sea and sand' holidays being taken to Spain and there has been a growth in rural and cultural tourism. Also, tourists are taking more short breaks in Spain rather than visiting the country for their main annual holiday.

The modern tourist to Spain today is not only looking for a typical package holiday at the cheapest price, but rather a more holistic experience that includes all sorts of additional activities. These tourists are more self-sufficient when booking their holidays, increasingly using the internet, comparing prices, expecting quality and are altogether more sophisticated and demanding.

and Portugal. As the figures above for inbound tourism to Spain suggest, there was a rapid increase in the number of package holidays taken by United Kingdom residents during this period.

The reasons for this trend included:

- The increasing accessibility of European destinations – this was mainly provided through air travel, but the development of the European motorway network meant that coach travel to Spain, in particular, was increasingly possible;

- A growing number of United Kingdom tour operators developing package holidays, sold through high street travel agents – throughout this period, more coastal regions of Spain, as well as the Balearic Islands (Majorca, Minorca and Ibiza) and other countries, were developing tourist resorts. Tour operators were quick to seize the commercial opportunities presented to them;

- Taking package holidays became increasingly affordable and fashionable for United Kingdom outbound tourists – many people found that there was little difference between the prices for domestic holidays and those charged for package holidays abroad;

- Mediterranean areas have guaranteed sunshine and good weather throughout the main holiday period in the summer months, whereas the British climate is less predictable, the temperature of the sea cooler and the chance of rainfall higher;

- European mass tourism resorts catered well for the United Kingdom market, providing the same range of food and drink popular in United Kingdom resorts. Package holidaymakers were generally happy to be able to buy fish and chips and drink the same

brands of beer that they could at home. English was a commonly-spoken language and package tourists felt comfortable with the culture of the mass tourism resorts.

The trend of increasing numbers of package holidays to mass tourism resorts continued into the 1980s. During the period from the 1960s into the 1980s, the impact of tourism on the environment and culture of the tourist resorts which experienced mass tourism was not given much consideration. Package holidays were relatively cheap and an increasing range of choice was available, with destinations such as Cyprus, Turkey and even Tunisia in north Africa developing resorts to cater for mass tourism. Destinations such as Ibiza and Magaluf on Majorca were associated with somewhat unruly behaviour and became as famous for their night life as much as for the beaches and guaranteed sunshine.

Destinations south of the Mediterranean, such as Tenerife and Gran Canaria, also developed as some

Even today some resorts have tourist shops catering for the English-speaking United Kingdom market

groups of tourists wished to keep their distance from those areas that were developing a poor reputation.

By the 1980s, the package holiday market had become relatively sophisticated with a range of destinations available as well as an increasingly wide choice of accommodation grades. More up-market accommodation became available, although the majority of tourists were still staying in hotels. Also, new package holiday products were developed for different client groups. Singles holidays, family-centred resorts and other types of products became available. Tour operators were still able to sell their holidays through high-street travel agents and the operators produced brochures aimed at different sections of their market.

In 1977 a significant development in the travel and tourism industry was the introduction of the Skytrain flights to New York operated by Sir Freddie Laker. The Skytrain was the first generation of low-cost airlines and operated between London and New York. Tickets were sold on a 'first come, first served' basis at a price far below what the major airlines offered. Freddie Laker's planes flew full of passengers.

When the flight was full, passengers waited for the next flight! This was a very different experience from transatlantic air travel up until that time, where passenger comfort was seen as paramount and champagne was regularly served on flights. The Skytrain was only in business for a few years. The larger airlines managed to force Sir Freddie out of business and he was bankrupt in 1982. However, from that time, air travel to the United States became more affordable and as had happened previously in Europe, more and more people of ordinary means could consider taking a long-haul holiday to visit New York or possibly one of the mass tourism destinations in Florida.

Industry Info...

Club 18-30

This was typical of how the package holiday market to mass tourism resorts became more specialised. The company specialises in cut-price holidays for young people, with the average age of its clients being 21. About one-third of the people taking Club 18-30 holidays are taking their first holiday abroad without their parents.

The company has received a great deal of adverse publicity regarding the notorious image of the sometimes irresponsible behaviour of its clients. However, it appeared that this reputation merely helped to boost sales. Resorts such as Ayia Napa in Cyprus, San Antonio in Ibiza and Faliraki in Rhodes have become associated with the Club 18-30 image.

Club 18-30 is still trading on its reputation of giving young people a good time, as the extract from the 2008 online information below suggests.

'Welcome to the 2008 Club 18-30 holiday experience. A unique fusion of brilliant holidays and fantastic party people. All day. All night. All together! That's the essence of the Club 18-30 holiday experience. But with the option to do your own thing whenever!'

www.thomascook.com

Skytrain made New York an accessible destination for a greater number of tourists

4.3 Activity holidays and winter sports

The growth of package holidays to Mediterranean beach resorts continued into the 1980s and beyond. The traditional package holiday was based around a hotel situated near a beach, which typically had a swimming pool and other facilities. Many holidaymakers were happy to soak up the sun and enjoy the warm waters of the Mediterranean or the heated pool provided by the hotel. On this type of holiday evening entertainment was usually provided and some people chose to visit night clubs and discos into the early hours, with day times spent relaxing in the sun.

However, since the 1980s, there has been a rise in the number of activity or special interest holidays. There are a number of reasons for this:

1. The trend of increased leisure time and continued affluence means that more United Kingdom residents can afford more than one holiday per year;

2. Although the main summer holiday is often still taken as a package, more people are looking for something different on a second holiday;

3. The travel industry has aircraft and hotel capacity available all year round and is looking for new commercial opportunities;

4. Some holidaymakers are increasingly looking for an alternative to the sun, sea and sand holiday concept;

5. New tour operators have become specialised in offering specific types of holiday to small sections of the market (niche markets);

6. Tourism authorities at established summer destinations are keen to develop activities that would attract tourists outside of the main holiday season;

7. As in other areas of the travel and tourism industry, working-class people found that they could enjoy taking part in activities that previously only rich people could afford;

8. Some tourists have become more discerning and have been looking for a more rewarding experience while on holiday, rather than just relaxing by a beach. The United Kingdom outbound and domestic tourist market is changing and becoming more sophisticated. The needs and expectations of tourists are continually changing and becoming more demanding.

Participation in winter sports has become possible for more people from the 1980s onwards

Activity and special interest holidays

An activity or special interest holiday is simply a holiday where a significant proportion of the holiday is spent undertaking a specific activity. The holidaymaker is involved in the activity along with other people who share the same interest. There are a limitless number of activity or special interest holidays available, from archaeology holidays to wine tasting, and it is not easy to break down the range of holidays into clear groups.

Very broadly, activity and special interest holidays can be subdivided into sporting holidays and cultural holidays. Sporting holidays include:

- Cricket tours;
- Cycling holidays;
- Fishing holidays;

- Golf holidays;
- Motor racing;
- Rock climbing;
- Skiing and other winter sports;
- Tennis;
- Walking tours.

The list above is just a small selection of sports that could be played during a special interest holiday. However, it is important to understand that watching or participating in the sport is the main reason for taking part in the holiday. Playing one round of golf during a week's stay at a beach hotel is not seen as a special interest holiday.

Golf holidays are a popular type of special interest sporting holiday

Cultural holidays include:

- Bird watching;
- Botany/naturalist;
- Cooking;

- Photography;
- Religious/pilgrimages;
- Safaris;
- Wine tasting.

Again, the list above is just a small selection of the range of cultural special interest holidays available and, as before, it is important to appreciate that the majority of the time on the holiday should be taken up with the main activity.

Sailing on a traditional ship off the coast of Vietnam would be seen as an activity holiday

Bird watching is a very popular form of special interest or activity holiday

It is common to include camping, caravanning, driving motor homes and canal or river cruising in a classification of activity holidays. All of these holidays require participants to be involved practically in activities such as erecting tents and cooking, or setting sails and steering a vessel. All of these activities are seen as part of the fun of the holiday and people who choose this type of holiday often prefer to stay on camping and caravan sites or on board ships and boats rather than stay in a hotel.

Many modern campsites have a wide range of facilities, but for some people, camping on basic sites with minimal facilities is still attractive. It is very much a matter of choice and those choosing this type of holiday are looking for a different experience from merely enjoying the facilities of a hotel.

Camping and caravanning is not limited to domestic tourism. Since the 1970s, more and more tourists have chosen to use campsites in European countries, usually by taking a cross-channel ferry and driving to their chosen destination. Since 1995, the Channel Tunnel has provided an alternative means of taking a car to Europe.

Camping is extremely popular in France and Spain, with good quality campsites readily available in all

Being 'close to nature' is one of the attractions of caravan and camping holidays

tourist areas. Driving to many areas of France and other European countries is made easy by the excellent system of roads, with relatively less congestion than in the United Kingdom. Holidays where tourists drive their own vehicles to a destination are known as self-drive holidays. One of the advantages of doing this is that the holidaymaker is not restricted to a specific amount of luggage, as they would be if they were travelling by air. It is common to attach a roof rack or trailer to a car to increase the amount of equipment or luggage that can be carried.

Some tourists choose to take their own equipment, although driving to a campsite, where the tent is already erected and all equipment is supplied is also a possibility. Camping is often seen as a good choice for family holidays where children as well as adults can enjoy the facilities provided on a campsite.

Industry Info...

Keycamp

Keycamp is one of a number of companies offering holidays to campsites in a range of European countries. Eurocamp, Canvas Holidays and Haven are companies that offer similar products.

Keycamp offers holidays on campsites in a number of European countries, including France, Switzerland, Slovenia and Italy. A recent development is that the company also offers camping holidays to Florida in the USA. This allows budget-conscious holidaymakers to access the attractions of central Florida at a lower price than would be charged for hotel accommodation.

Another aspect of product development for Keycamp and similar companies is the increasing range of accommodation available. Originally, the only type of accommodation on site was a frame tent, which included a kitchen area with fridge and bedrooms. More recently, campsites on the continent offer a range of mobile homes, cabins and chalets, and these have been added to the Keycamp range.

www.keycamp.co.uk

Winter sports holidays

Like many other aspects of the travel and tourism industry, winter sports holidays were originally only taken by affluent people who could afford to travel to fairly remote alpine villages during the winter months. As with other tourism developments, it was rail travel that made alpine resorts accessible. Resorts in the Alps where winter sports were originally developed, such as Zermatt, Chamonix and St Moritz, relied very heavily on railways to provide transport for their visitors. Up until about 30 years ago, many people in the United Kingdom would not have considered taking a winter sports holiday, on account of the cost involved. However, due to a combination of reasons, including the growth of low-cost airlines, winter sports holidays have steadily increased in popularity. Other reasons that have resulted in more people taking skiing holidays are the emergence of new resorts, developments by tour operators, better accessibility of ski resorts and the growth of new activities, for example snow boarding.

Swiss mountain railways were very significant in the development of winter sports resorts

New ski resorts

From the 1970s onwards, a new generation of Alpine winter sports resorts were developed. These include Tinges, Les Arcs, Les Deux Alps, L'Alpe D'Huez, Valmorel and Avoriaz. These resorts contain hotels and apartment accommodation, and were built at high altitudes, which guaranteed good skiing conditions for most of the season. The infrastructure of lifts and cable cars was developed at the same time, providing a wide range of skiing for all levels of ability.

The provision of a good system of chairlifts, draglifts and cable cars makes skiing more accessible

Tour operators

UK-based tour operators began to offer package holidays to winter sports resorts from the early 1970s. All of the elements required for package holidays were present and tour operators were able to provide packages that included not only accommodation and flights, but equipment hire and lessons. Some of these companies began to specialise in group travel and began offering ski holidays to schools for the first time. For many United Kingdom residents who took up skiing and other winter sports, their first experience was on a school ski trip. More recently, winter sports holidays to Canada and the USA have become popular as cheaper flights and good snow records make these destinations an attractive alternative.

Many experienced skiers today had their first experience of winter sports holidays on a school ski trip

Accessibility

The 1970s and 1980s saw a significant development in the network of motorways across France and other European countries. This meant that it was far easier to access winter sports resorts by road transport. Consequently, transfers from airports to resorts were easier and it also became increasingly possible to travel to winter sports resorts by coach or even car. Many

French resorts can be reached in about 10 hours driving time from Calais so it became feasible to travel to the resort by coach, normally travelling overnight.

Changing tastes and fashion

As winter sports holidays became more accessible, they became more fashionable. More United Kingdom residents could afford to take a second holiday each year and many were looking for an alternative to the summer sun package holiday. Increasing numbers of people recognised how enjoyable winter sports activities could be and welcomed the opportunity to spend a week in a completely different environment, such as a high alpine resort. To a certain extent, decreasing amounts of snowfall in the United Kingdom contributed to this. Over time, new winter sports activities, in particular snow boarding, attracted a new generation of enthusiasts to winter sports resorts in the Alps and other European resort areas.

People appreciate the opportunity to spend time in mountain environments when taking winter sports holidays

The development of low-cost airlines

In the 1990s, the emergence of low-cost airlines such as easyJet and Ryanair meant that it became even more possible to travel to winter sports resorts independently and relatively cheaply. Increasing numbers of people could book their flights using the internet and make their own travel arrangements, rather than making use of the services of a tour operator. Additionally, it became more feasible for United Kingdom residents to purchase apartments and other accommodation in winter sports resorts, allowing them to consider skiing for weekends or to visit winter sports resorts several times each year.

4.4 Short break holidays

Short breaks are essentially a holiday that lasts for less than four nights. In fact, a holiday of one night away from home can technically be called a short break. Usually, a short break involves a holiday of between two and four nights away. Again, one of the major reasons for the development of short break holidays was that increasing numbers of United Kingdom residents found they had sufficient holiday entitlement to consider a second or even a third holiday each year. They were also able to afford the additional holidays.

Other reasons for the growth of short break holidays include transport developments, such as the opening of the Channel Tunnel and the rise of low-cost airlines offering short-haul and domestic flights. This meant that destinations on the near continent and other regions of the United Kingdom became increasingly accessible for

Industry Info...

Eurostar

Short breaks to Paris and Brussels have grown in popularity since the introduction of the Eurostar service. These trains have been in operation since November 1994 and allow passengers to travel from the centre of London to the centre of Paris or Brussels in under three hours, making short breaks to these cities much more feasible.

Until recently, the London Eurostar services ran from Waterloo Station. However with the completion of the High Speed 1 railway line in the autumn of 2007, Eurostar services have been transferred to the re-developed St Pancras International Station. The completion of the High Speed 1 line reduced journey times between the two cities even more. The scheduled journey time from London St Pancras to the Gard du Nord in Paris is now just 2 hours and 15 minutes, and Brussels can be reached in under 2 hours.

In addition, the Eurostar service runs to Disneyland Paris in just over two and a half hours. All of these destinations have become feasible for short breaks since the introduction of the Eurostar service using the Channel Tunnel.

www.eurostar.com

Central Paris can now be reached in less than two and a half hours from London using the Eurostar service

a short break away from home. For example, cities such as Belfast and Edinburgh became accessible from the south of the United Kingdom and affordable using low-cost carriers.

Also, tour operators began to package city breaks and other short break destinations as they had with Mediterranean holidays in the past. Other travel and tourism organisations, such as accommodation providers, also saw an opportunity to create special deals for people wanting to stay for two, three or four nights. This, of course, was a far cry from the days when nearly every holiday was for either 7 or 14 days, starting and finishing on a Saturday!

It is simply not possible to list every type of short break holiday. Many sporting holidays and activity holidays are short breaks, because they last usually less than one week. Similarly, visits to National Parks for weekend breaks over Bank Holiday weekends to take part in activities, such as walking or cycling, can be classed as short breaks.

Walking holidays in National Parks are often taken as short breaks

4.5 Long-haul destinations

Long-haul destinations are essentially those that require a flight outside of Europe which lasts more than four or five hours. The precise amount of time the flight takes is not as important as the fact that the traveller is visiting a destination further away than European destinations to which the only reasonable method of travel is by air. Thus, all destinations in North America, Asia and the Middle East are long-haul destinations. The growth of travel by United Kingdom residents to long-haul destinations really began with the arrival of the Laker Skytrain in the late 1970s. Freddie Laker challenged the monopoly of the major airlines and began the process of making transatlantic travel affordable for many more people.

At about the same time, governments were considering how to allow more airlines to support the development of air travel. International rules governing air travel were, up until the 1980s, extremely complicated and restricted the number of airlines that could take off, fly over and land in different countries. Certain airlines, called 'flag carriers', such as British Airways and Air France, were given preferential treatment which restricted competition and kept fares relatively high. In the 1980s, governments in North America and Europe began introducing deregulation and developing 'open skies' agreements, which allowed more airlines to operate, encouraged competition and reduced fares for customers. Open skies policies in Europe led the way for the development of the low-cost carriers.

Thus, as with so many other developments in the travel and tourism industry, more and more United Kingdom residents found that they were able to afford to visit North America, with a steady growth in the number of United Kingdom residents visiting North America in the 1970s and 1980s. Following Freddie Laker's ill-fated attempt to provide low-cost travel, new airlines such as Virgin Atlantic and British Midland began operating regular flights to North America, competing with British Airways. American-based airlines flying transatlantic routes now include:

- American Airlines;
- Continental Airlines;
- United Airlines;
- US Airlines;
- North West Airlines;
- Delta Airlines.

In addition, within the last year the Canadian low-cost airline Zoom has begun flying to the USA. Also, European airlines offer indirect flights to North America and it is possible to fly to the United States indirectly via a Canadian city such as Toronto.

So, the potential tourist has a great deal of choice of which long-haul destinations to visit and, in the last few years, online travel companies such as Expedia and lastminute.com have provided an online booking facility that enables a very simple comparison of the schedules and prices available. This was not the case thirty years ago!

Industry Info...

United Kingdom arrivals in the USA

United Kingdom tourist arrivals into the United States showed a steady increase through the 1990s but the World Trade Centre attack in 2001 had a significant effect on visitor numbers.

Year	Number of Arrivals
1994	2,772,000
1995	2,888,000
1996	3,246,000
1997	3,721,000
1998	3,975,000
1999	4,252,000
2000	4,703,000
2001	4,097,000
2002	3,817,000
2003	3,936,000
2004	4,303,000
2005	4,345,000

The vast majority of United Kingdom residents who visit the United States head for one of four states. Together, in 2005, the states of Florida, New York, California and Nevada attracted over 90% of the United Kingdom visitors to the USA.

Florida (34.3%) – attracts UK visitors to the Disney and Universal Studios theme parks of Orlando, as well as to the Gulf Coast and the Kennedy Space Center. The warm climate makes Florida a virtually all-year-round destination.

New York (27.8%) – the majority of visitors to New York State actually visit New York City. In fact, 26.9% of UK visitors to the United States go to New York City. People are attracted by the iconic attractions such as the Empire State Building, the Statue of Liberty and Central Park, as well as the shopping facilities and the wide range of cultural attractions and museums.

Central Park is one of the major attractions in New York City

California (17.9%) – the two 'mega-cities' of Los Angeles and San Francisco attract many visitors, as well as Yosemite and other National Parks. The Hollywood and Beverley Hills areas of Los Angeles are particularly popular.

The Hollywood 'Walk of Fame' is extremely popular

Las Vegas provides a spectacular range of attractions

Nevada (10.3%) – by far the most popular destination within the state of Nevada is the city of Las Vegas. People are drawn by the casino-hotels, which provide 24-hour gambling and a wide range of other attractions, such as circus shows and the magical Bellagio fountains.

Las Vegas

As well as the USA, Canada is also a popular long-haul destination for United Kingdom visitors. In particular, tourists are drawn to the Toronto area of Ontario from where they can make a visit to the world-famous Niagara Falls and to the Canadian Rockies, where resorts such as Banff and Lake Louise are popular. Both in the USA and Canada, increasing numbers of United Kingdom visitors are now taking winter sports holidays, as well as visiting the countries in the summer months.

As well as the decreasing price of flights to North America, long-haul travel to other destinations was also

Niagara Falls is a world-famous attraction on the border between Canada and the United States

made more possible by a number of other reasons. Firstly, aircraft technology has continued to develop, and since the introduction of the Boeing 747 Jumbo Jet in the early 1970s, aircraft have been able to fly longer distances carrying more passengers. The 747 has a range of over 7,700 miles and can carry over 500 passengers on two decks. The recently-introduced Airbus A380 is the first larger aircraft with a longer range than the Jumbo Jet, which started flying thirty years ago.

Secondly, there are regions of the world that are now accessible to tourists which could only be visited with great difficulty in the recent past. The fall of Communism has led former Communist countries to accept tourists. This is especially true in China and other parts of South East Asia, which were extremely difficult to visit twenty years ago.

Also, more people have been able to afford long-haul

The Great Wall of China is now far more accessible for United Kingdom tourists

holidays that last three or more weeks. Destinations such as India, Australia and New Zealand have become increasingly popular amongst older people, who can take longer holidays in their retirement, as well as with younger backpackers.

As with other types of holiday, tour operators have developed a range of products to provide for people looking to visit long-haul destinations. These vary from fly-drive holidays in the USA and Canada, to escorted tours in less accessible areas of South America. Some tour operators, such as Kuoni, specialise in long-haul destinations, and there are a number of niche operators specialising in organising tours to specific destinations.

As well as an increase in leisure tourism to long-haul destinations, there has also been a corresponding increase in the number of people travelling for business

Sydney appeals to a wide range of tourists

reasons and to visit friends and relatives. There has been a steady increase in the number of multinational companies that have offices throughout the world, and it is more common now for business people to travel to long-haul destinations for conferences, meetings and trade fairs. Also, an increasing number of United Kingdom residents have friends and relatives living in a number of long-haul destinations. There is a steady flow of VFR (visiting friends and relatives) tourism between the United Kingdom and countries in the Indian sub-continent and it is more common to visit friends and relatives in Australia and New Zealand than it was in the past.

Finally, it must be remembered that not all long-haul travel is outbound. Increasing numbers of tourists from India, China and other countries are making visits to the United Kingdom.

4.6 Independent holidays and self-packaging

Independent travel is when tourists make their own bookings directly with airlines, accommodation providers and other travel and tourism organisations, rather than booking package holidays through a travel agent or tour operator. It does not mean that people are travelling more on their own. Self-packaging refers to the process of making a holiday booking by buying the components of a holiday as individual items and making a package in the same way that a tour operator would Increasingly, these purchases are made online, although it is still possible to buy the components of the holiday individually using a travel agent or possibly through a call centre.

It is common to arrange flights first and then to make accommodation bookings. Travel insurance, transfers, car hire and other travel products can all be purchased easily online, as and when required. However, the traveller does not have the assurance that the arrangements have been made by a professional travel agent and he or she may be liable for any mistakes made, such as booking flights or accommodation for the wrong dates. Also, these arrangements are not covered by the Package Travel Regulations, which can provide compensation if things go wrong with the travel arrangements.

Over recent years there has been a growth in independent travel and self-packaging at the expense of the traditional package holiday. There are a number of reasons for the growth in the number of independent holidays, including:

- More tourists are confident travellers who are used to visiting other countries, including long-haul destinations,

- More tourists do not feel that the products provided by tour operators meet their precise needs or have been disappointed with the experience of a package holiday in the past;

- Tourists find it more pleasurable to construct a trip based around what they particularly want to do, see and visit, rather than accepting a product that might not quite meet their needs;

- Those people who own properties abroad or who visit friends and relatives only need to make flight bookings since other components of the trip are already arranged;

- Tourists have far more information available to them

in order to research destinations before they travel. There is a greater range of guide books than ever before and a variety of websites that give reports and advice on accommodation and other travel products;

- Most importantly, the internet has made it possible to make travel bookings online, rather than being obliged to use the services of the travel agent. The internet provides independent travellers with the information they require and the means to book the flights and accommodation online at a time that is convenient to them.

Industry Info...

Trip Advisor

Trip Advisor is one of a new generation of web sites that offers reviews about accommodation provided by people who have stayed in the accommodation, as well as hosting an online booking facility. Some independent travellers welcome the opportunity to read what other people say about accommodation before they make a booking.

However, this type of web site has received some criticism. Accommodation providers feel that only people who have had a bad experience will be inclined to write reviews and these are likely to be critical. Also, there are suggestions that some accommodation providers are submitting critical reviews about their competitors!

www.tripadvisor.com

One of the principal reasons for the growth of self-packaging to short-haul destinations has been the development of low-cost or budget airlines such as flybe and bmibaby. As mentioned previously, these airlines now carry millions of passengers each year and have grown extremely rapidly over the last decade. Their rise has been very much associated with the increased use of the internet to make travel bookings. A greater proportion of people are now able to access the internet from their own homes using high-speed modems, facilitating easy access to the websites of the airlines. When accessing the website of a low-cost airline, the cost of each flight available between the chosen destinations is displayed. The traveller can then choose which flight to take and the precise cost of the chosen flight will be calculated in seconds. The flight can be purchased immediately because the website of the airline is linked to the web site of the credit or debit card company. An email is sent with a specific code and the traveller only has to take this to the airport – no tickets are issued. A recent development is that the low-

More people are self-packaging holidays to winter sports destinations with low-cost airlines

cost airlines are encouraging travellers to check-in online and not to take hold baggage on to the flight. Travellers doing this will find that their flights are slightly cheaper, since the airline saves operating costs.

Most travel products are now available to be purchased online and it is a very straightforward process to make reservations for flights and accommodation bookings. However, for more specialised travel, perhaps involving large groups or when travelling to more exotic destinations, travel agents and tour operators will still be used. Likewise, booking complicated itineraries involving internal flights within certain countries will still be more likely to be booked through travel agents.

Internal flights within certain countries are more likely to be booked through travel agents

4.7 Impacts of tourism and sustainable tourism

Over the last twenty years there has been a growing awareness of the impact tourism has on the environment and societies in holiday destinations. As mass tourism first developed along the Spanish coastal areas (costas) and other areas around the Mediterranean, there was little concern for the negative impacts that tourism was having on the environment of the area or on the lives of the people living there. This was not considered to be as important as the short-term positive impacts created by tourism, such as increased employment opportunities and income for local residents and businesses operating in the area. However, over time, it was seen how the sudden growth in tourist numbers brought negative impacts as well as positive. Concurrently, concepts such as ecotourism, responsible tourism and sustainable tourism have evolved. This is as a result of more research being undertaken into the range of impacts tourism creates and the ways in which these impacts can be managed more carefully, so that the benefits of tourism are maximised while the negative impacts are reduced.

It is common to classify the positive and negative impacts of tourism under the following headings:

- Economic impacts;
- Environmental impacts;
- Social impacts;
- Cultural impacts.

Economic impacts – positive

Tourism generates revenue for a variety of businesses

Throughout the world, it is believed that providing tourists with information about the area they are visiting is likely to make them behave in a more responsible manner

Are actors in a stunt show at a theme park working in the tourism industry?

and creates a wide range of employment opportunities. At the global scale, tourism is seen as one of the world's largest and fastest-growing industries. The World Tourism Organisation is anticipating that in 2007 there will have been nearly 900 million international tourist arrivals, each spending money on transport, accommodation and other tourism products and services. This upward trend has continued throughout the last 50 years.

Within the United Kingdom, it is estimated that inbound tourism generates around £16 billion each year. More importantly, domestic tourism, including day trips and staying visits, generates over £60 billion per year. In terms of employment, it is estimated that in the United Kingdom 1.4 million jobs are directly related to tourism and there are over 600,000 jobs related to tourism activity. It is not easy to calculate the precise number

of jobs directly and indirectly related to tourism. This is mainly because it is not easy to identify to what extent some jobs are related to the travel and tourism industry. Coach drivers would be identified as being tourism jobs, but some coach drivers do work that is not related to tourism, such as taking children to school or providing

Over 3,000 jobs in Bournemouth are related to tourist accommodation

Industry Info...

The value of tourism in Bournemouth

Bournemouth is one of the leading coastal resorts in the United Kingdom. The resort received just over 1.2 million staying visitors in 2005. There was a total of over 4.5 million nights spent in Bournemouth by visitors. These visitors spent just over £294 million in total. In addition, there were calculated to be over 3 million day visitors who spent over £132 million in the resort.

It was also calculated that in 2005, about 12,700 jobs in Bournemouth were related to tourism, accounting for approximately 16% of all employment in the town.

www.bournemouth.gov.uk

transport for workers. Also, is the person who maintains the coaches working in tourism or not?

As well as generating employment and income, another positive economic impact of tourism is improvements in infrastructure. These include road and rail improvements, airport development and improvements in utilities, such as water supply and telecommunications. Through these, local people can benefit from the improved facilities that have been provided for tourists. Another economic benefit of tourism is referred to as the 'multiplier effect'. This is the process whereby money that is spent by tourists in an

area is re-circulated in the local economy and is actually worth more than its face value. For example, the wages paid to a hotel waiter will be spent on goods and services in local shops. In turn, the local shopkeepers will spend the money they receive from customers on local goods and services, and so the process continues. Also, other businesses prosper as an indirect result of increased tourism, such as more builders being needed to build more tourist accommodation, thus creating even more jobs in the area.

Economic impacts – negative

Very often an influx of visitors into an area pushes up the price of goods and services, meaning that local people have to pay more for food, drinks, transport etc. It is often the case that in popular tourist areas retail shops provide products for tourists more than they do for local people, meaning that more gift shops and restaurants might open at the expense of shops providing basic goods and services for people living in the area.

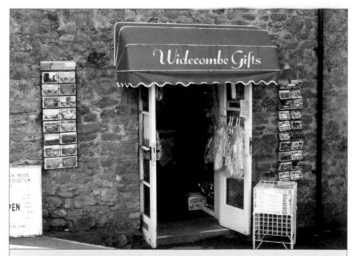

Gift shops are common in tourist areas, but do not provide goods and services for local people

Local people often have to pay additional taxes to help finance services provided for tourists, such as water treatment facilities and tourist information centres. Some holiday areas have a large number of second homes that are only used for short periods of the year by their owners. This is particularly the case in National Parks and popular coastal areas. The demand for second homes often increases the prices of all housing in the area, making it more difficult for local people, especially young people, to buy their first property. Second home ownership is an example of a negative economic impact of tourism, which may be a cause of conflict between local people and visitors to an area.

Second homes are popular in many tourist areas

One of the most significant negative economic impacts of tourism is the decline in traditional employment which happens when workers move from industries such as farming, mining and fishing into service jobs in the tourism industry. This was one of the first negative impacts identified in Spain and Greece in the 1970s and 1980s, during the period of the rapid growth in

package holidays to Mediterranean areas. During this time, many workers left jobs on the land and at sea to work in the tourism industry, which had better working conditions.

In some Alpine areas, traditional skills are in danger of being lost as more people are attracted to jobs in tourism

Although jobs in tourism may have better conditions than jobs on the land, tourism employment is sometimes seen as being poorly paid, so although there may be an increase in employment, these jobs are often, but by no means always, relatively poorly paid. Additionally, many tourism jobs tend to be seasonal and involve working anti-social hours.

Another negative economic impact of tourism is over-dependency. It may be that, as tastes and fashions change or due to any of a range of external pressures, the number of tourists visiting a particular destination falls very suddenly, leading to a loss of employment and businesses closing. Terrorist activity, natural disasters and climate change are all beyond the control of the travel and tourism industry, and may result in a particular

Ski resorts are dependent on sufficient snowfall to attract skiers to the area

destination losing a significant proportion of its tourism income over a short period of time.

Finally, there is the issue of economic leakage. This happens when money bought into a destination through tourism 'leaks' away from the area. For example, many hotels in tourism destinations in less economically developed countries (LEDCs) are not owned by local companies and senior staff may not be local people. Thus, a significant proportion of the money paid by tourists to stay in the hotel does not find its way into the local economy, but instead is 'leaked' away back to other countries to pay shareholders of the hotel companies and tour opertors.

Environmental impacts – positive

It is generally the case that tourism has created more negative impacts on the environment than positive impacts. However, increasing awareness of the need for careful environmental management has helped to

Many hotels in coastal areas in LEDCs may not be owned by local companies

Turning former industrial sites into museums can help to improve the environment of the area

reduce the negative impacts of tourism in recent years. There are a number of ways in which tourism can have a positive impact on the environment of a destination and in some cases can be a force for environmental change. In the United Kingdom, for example, a number of former industrial sites and areas of derelict land have been preserved and developed as tourist attractions, and stretches of disused canals have been renovated so that they can be used for tourist purposes. Similarly, tourism can also promote increased funding for renovation work on historic buildings such as castles, churches and cathedrals in order to ensure that they are preserved for future generations.

Preservation work on historic buildings in tourism destinations is one of the positive environmental impacts of tourism

Environmental impacts – negative

It has to be accepted that many forms of travel have a damaging impact on the environment. Trains, cars, aircraft and ships all consume fuel and produce emissions that cause atmospheric pollution which, in turn, contributes to climate change. In recent years there has been a growing acceptance of the harmful environmental impacts of travel, and more measures are now being taken to help reduce the impacts. These include making aircraft and vehicles more fuel efficient, increasing the use of recyclable materials in the construction of vehicles and aircraft, and experimenting with new types of fuel. In an increasing number of destinations, such as historic cities and National Parks, schemes are being introduced to reduce the amount of pollution and congestion caused by motor vehicles. These include park and ride schemes and a number of initiatives to encourage visitors to use public transport instead of their cars.

In Zion Canyon National Park in Utah USA, no vehicles are allowed in the park and all visitors are transported by electric buses

As well as environmental pollution caused by travel and traffic, air pollution also causes damage to buildings and noise pollution is an issue in busy resorts with a vibrant night life. Additionally, pollution is caused by

tourists producing litter. This creates an eyesore on the landscape as well as being a threat to the safety of people and animals. Water pollution is another common issue that has been addressed in recent years. In the past, many beaches were unsafe partly because untreated or partially-treated sewage was allowed to enter the sea adjacent to the beaches. The European Union Blue Flag Beach initiative has encouraged many local authorities to take measures to reduce effluent and pollution, so that their beaches can be considered for the blue flag status.

Congestion and overcrowding are also commonly identified as negative environmental impacts of tourism. Congestion is normally applied to the

Rubbish and litter on beaches is unsightly and a threat to the safety of people and animals

problems associated with too many cars being within or travelling to a destination. It is common for popular destinations in the United Kingdom to be congested on Bank Holidays and during peak holiday periods and there are constant reports about motorways being congested on summer weekends as holidaymakers leave home to travel to popular tourist destinations. Overcrowding occurs where the volume of visitors at a destination increases to a point at which the enjoyment of the destination is spoilt. This can occur when there are too many people on a beach, walking around an historic town or trying to reach a viewpoint at a natural attraction.

It could be argued that the Skywalk project at the Grand Canyon is an inappropriate development, despite attracting more visitors to the area and providing additional income to Native American Indians

Too many tourists walking along streets in an historic town can spoil the visit

The final category of negative environmental impact is about destroying the natural landscape of an area. This includes the process of erosion caused by walkers, horse-riders and other users, the loss of habitats for plants and animals, as well as the spoiling of the natural landscape with inappropriate development.

Social impacts – positive

One of the major motivating factors for travel is to meet new people and learn about different cultures. Travel and tourism often leads to a greater understanding between people living in different societies. Very often, tourists benefit from new and improved facilities that are provided for tourists. This may include improvements to infrastructure, such as roads and water supply, as well as attractions, accommodation and catering facilities – there is nothing stopping people living in a tourist destination from enjoying themselves in restaurants or visiting attractions built mainly for tourist use.

Tourists will often gain a greater respect for the lifestyle of the people living in the area they are visiting.

Increased tourism also leads to local communities improving their skills and improving their social status. In well-managed tourism developments, local people are encouraged to undertake education and training to enable them to feel part of the tourist development, thereby better appreciating the economic benefits that tourism brings.

At the Grand Canyon West development, the Indian chief has been trained to be a tour guide and to provide off-road tours of the area

Social impacts – negative

There are a number of negative social impacts of tourism that have been identified. These are mainly related to conflict between the tourists and the host community (the people living in the tourist destination). These may result from the behaviour of people living in the area who resent the tourists taking over their community. However, it is arguably more common that anti-social behaviour from groups of tourists will be the cause of conflict. Negative social impacts may also include increased crime in the area, such as prostitution, illegal gambling, drug dealing and robbery.

Very often, this is not related to local people, but occurs as a result of criminal gangs moving into the area to exploit tourists and sometimes local people as well. In some destinations, local people have been obliged to move away from where they have traditionally lived to make way for tourism development. This is called the 'displacement effect' and often causes resentment towards tourists and developers.

In some coastal areas of Spain, local people have had to make way for the development of apartments and golf complexes

Another common issue is the matter of seasonal employment, or more realistically, unemployment. In destinations that have a marked peak in the number of tourists at a certain period of the year, there is a significant rise in the amount of unemployment during those times of the year when the number of tourists visiting the area decreases. Many tourist areas are developing strategies to maintain a flow of visitors throughout the year, thus reducing the impact of seasonal unemployment.

These issues are more commonly demonstrated in areas of mass tourism, in larger cities and in certain destinations within the less-developed world. Conversely, there are many destinations where there is little or no conflict between local people and tourists.

Cultural impacts – positive

It would be nice to feel that tourism is a force for good in contributing to the cultural heritage and activities within destinations. It may also help to preserve traditional customs such as music, dance and theatre, as well as creating a demand for locally-produced foods and drink. Tourism can also stimulate the production and sale of local arts and crafts to meet the needs of visitors and, at the same time, contribute to the continuation of traditional craft skills. Tourism also has an important role to play in reinforcing a region's cultural identity.

Peruvian Indian women welcoming visitors in a traditional manner and wearing traditional costume

Cultural impacts – negative

It is increasingly considered that the negative impacts of tourism on culture are, in the long term, more significant than its harmful environmental impacts. Whereas environmental impacts can be corrected with proper management techniques, once the cultural heritage of an area is lost, it may never be retrieved. More people now recognise that tourism may bring about a dilution or loss of an area's cultural identity, especially in destinations that have seen a rapid development of mass tourism.

In destinations, it is sometimes easier to provide international food and drink with which tourists are familiar rather than to encourage them to eat foods associated with the local area. This has not been helped by the global development of fast-food chains and multinational brands of drinks. This process is sometimes known as 'westernisation', as the values of visitors to different cultures become increasingly imposed on the local culture.

Another negative cultural impact of tourism is the staging of events, dance or music specifically for tourists in a way that demeans the local culture of the area. However, more and more tourists are becoming aware of their potential impact on the culture and heritage of the area they are visiting and people are less willing to support activities which exploit local traditions and culture.

Sustainable tourism

For the last 20 years or so there has been a growing recognition of the negative impacts that tourist activity has on the environment and societies in which it takes

Performing traditional dances for tourists could be seen as being demeaning to traditional culture

tourism takes place and on the culture of the people who live there. So, sustainable tourism is concerned with reducing the negative impacts of tourism and planning to increase the positive impacts. It also means that, in the longer term, the lifestyle and culture of the people living in the area are not adversely affected by tourism.

Sustainable tourism is a term which has been defined in a number of ways, each of which has a slightly different interpretation. Sustainable tourism is clearly related to sustainable development, the concept which recognises that the Earth's resources are finite, and that, unless certain steps are taken, these resources will run out. Thus it is necessary to preserve resources as much as possible, which is the essence of sustainable tourism.

A definition produced by the English Tourism Council (which no longer exists) in 2002 suggested that:

Providing boardwalks through ecologically-sensitive areas of forests prevent visitors from walking on the forest floor to help protect the vegetation and is a good example of sustainable tourism management

place. Although there is tremendous variation from destination to destination, there have been a number of examples where mass tourism has radically changed the culture of the society which lived in the area before tourism began to develop. In some locations, the environment has been changed significantly. This is nowhere more so than in the Mediterranean coastal regions, where what were once small fishing villages forty years ago are now massive resorts attracting millions of visitors each year.

Sustainable tourism is about meeting the needs of today's tourists without having a major long-term harmful effect on the environment of the area in which

135

'Sustainable tourism is about managing tourism's impacts on the environment, communities and the economy to make sure that the effects are positive rather than negative, for the benefit of future generations. It is a management approach that is relevant to all types of tourism, regardless of whether it takes place in cities, towns, the countryside or the coast'.

A number of forms of sustainable tourism have been identified:

- Economic sustainability is about ensuring that tourism businesses are profitable and provide appropriate employment for local people. It is not the case that sustainable tourism is about stopping people visiting an area. Tourism is increasingly seen as a vital source of income for many communities that rely on the income they receive from tourism to survive;

- Ecological sustainability relates to looking after the physical environment and maintaining the ecological diversity of an area;

Economic sustainability is supported through local people selling traditional hand-made products to tourists

Industry Info...

The Dartmoor National Park Authority (DNPA) – sustainable tourism strategies.

As with all National Parks, sustainable tourism development is seen as a priority for the DNPA. One of the functions of the DNPA is to look after the interests of the communities living on Dartmoor, and income from tourism is seen as being vital to the economy of the area.

The DNPA has produced a number of policies to promote sustainable tourism in the National Park. These include:

- Restricting all traffic in the park to 40 mph to reduce pollution and accidents involving the animals that graze on open pasture;

- Encouraging the use of public transport by making bus stops visible;

- Working with local businesses to develop a scheme encouraging sustainable practices called *The Dartmoor Charter for Sustainable Tourism*;

- Supporting local farmers by encouraging visitors to buy local produce;

- Supporting cyclists by providing cycle tracks, information and a 'freewheeler' bus service, which collects cyclists and allows them to cycle home without using their cars;

- Encouraging more people to stay in the National Park to support local accommodation providers.

www.dartmoor-npa.gov.uk

- Cultural sustainability is about supporting people who live in an area to maintain their culture. It involves ensuring that local people are consulted about tourism development plans and are not forced away from the land on which they live. Also, local people can be taught new skills to enable them to benefit from tourism.

Reducing the speed of road traffic reduces pollution and reduces the risk of accidents

Responsible and ecotourism

We have seen that sustainable tourism involves a set of policies and strategies to reduce the impacts of tourism on the environment and society, in order to ensure the long-term future of the areas in which tourism takes place through careful management and planning. Responsible tourism is about the actions of tourists and tourism organisations to support the principles of sustainable tourism. Responsible tourism is also referred to as ecotourism, alternative tourism and green tourism.

As with sustainable tourism, there are a number of definitions of responsible or ecotourism, each with a slightly different emphasis. One widely-used definition was devised by Honey in 1999, who's book was entitled 'Who Owns Paradise?' Honey defined ecotourists as people who:

'Travel to natural areas with a view to respecting, enjoying and being educated about the natural environment and the culture of the local community in a manner that is low-impact and sensitive to the long-term sustainability of these features.'

Ecotourism and responsible tourism are seen as a reaction to, or an alternative to, mass tourism, which has been shown to have very little respect for local culture and has had a significant impact on the environment of the areas in which it has developed. Seven basic principles of ecotourism or responsible tourism have been devised. These are:

1. Travelling to natural destinations
Ecotourism involves travelling to natural as opposed to purpose-built resort destinations, understanding the

Iceland is considered to be an ecotourism destination

natural history of the destination and causing as little impact on the destination as possible.

2. Developing environmental awareness
Ecotourism involves experiencing and learning about the natural environment.

3. Minimising impact
Ecotourism attempts to reduce the impacts of tourism and the consumption of resources through approaches such as:

- Using local building materials;
- Using renewable energy sources;
- Making use of recycling wherever possible;
- Reducing water consumption;
- Monitoring or limiting the number of visitors.

Visitors to National Parks in North America have to pay an entrance charge

4. Providing financial benefits for conservation
Ecotourism can provide funds for financing projects that support environmental management. This may include making a charge for tourists to visit natural attractions or to enter National Parks.

5. Providing financial benefits to the local community
Ecotourism involves reducing the amount of 'leakage' from the communities in which tourism takes place. The local community should benefit more and be involved in decisions relating to the planning and development of tourist facilities.

6. Respecting local culture
Ecotourism incorporates educating ecotourists about local customs, practices, dress-codes and appropriate behaviour. Ecotourists are more likely to purchase gifts and souvenirs which are locally produced, thereby providing direct employment for the local community.

7. Supporting human rights
The final aspect of ecotourism involves respecting human rights. This may involve not travelling to countries that have a poor record of human rights or exploitation of its people. It also involves not buying products made by people working in very poor conditions or practices that involve the exploitation of animals.

Tourism businesses and sustainable tourism

The changing attitude towards sustainable tourism and ecotourism does not only apply to tourists. Increasingly, tourism businesses need to be seen to be acting in a responsible manner and adopting sustainable practices.

Ecotourism involves respecting the religion and customs of local people

Buying fake designer goods, possibly made by people working in poor conditions for low wages, would not be seen as ecotourism

This can be evidenced in a number of ways. Increasingly, hotels ask guests to consider how many towels they use to reduce the need to wash the towels, which requires damaging detergents. Also, hotel rooms may well use a system where a key card is inserted before the lights can be turned on, thus reducing the amount of electricity used.

Tour operators are reducing the number of brochures they produce as well as asking customers to recycle brochures. This reduces the use of resources, as well as cutting costs for the operator. Nearly all tourism organisations carry statements about the companies' policy towards sustainable tourism on their websites. The majority of organisations now carry some form of 'corporate responsibility' statement. For example, the Thomas Cook group has a responsible tourism policy which covers care for the environment, looking after people, looking after heritage and raising awareness.

Industry Info...

easyJet – an extract from the company's environmental policy.

'Our new aircraft + full aircraft = less carbon dioxide than traditional aircraft'.

At easyJet we're committed to minimising our environmental impact, both in the air and on the ground.

That's why we:

- Invest in new technology to have one of the youngest, cleanest and quietest fleets in the world;

- Have the highest levels of environmental efficiency – flying with a traditional airline, on the same type of aircraft, emits 27% more fuel per passenger mile than flying with us;

- Have published our Environmental Code, to show we will monitor and reduce our environmental impact. It's our commitment to you and to the environment so you can hold us to account to make sure we deliver exactly what we say we will do in the air, on the ground and in the future.'

www.easyJet.com

Tourism businesses have been obliged to demonstrate that they are aware of their responsibilities in relation to sustainability and ecotourism. However, the primary objective of the majority of tourism organisations is to remain profitable and so the need to adopt sustainable practices and policies must be balanced against the need to remain profitable in a competitive environment. Also, new tourism companies and organisations have developed in recent years to provide products for those wishing to take part in ecotourism activities.

Industry Info...

Ecotravel.com

Ecotravel is one of a new breed of travel organisations which promotes ecotourism and makes use of internet technology. Ecotravel encourages travellers to share their experiences and by doing this Ecotravel expects to become a resource of information on travel to ecotourism destinations and taking part in ecotourism activities.

The *Ecotravel* website includes information on current topics relating to ecotourism, articles about ecotourism activities, tips for travellers, reviews about holidays taken and travel planning information.

More importantly, *Ecotravel* acts as a large database of ecotourism activities and destinations, so if the visitor to the site wishes to go whale watching in Canada, the site will provide information about companies offering whale watching trips.

www.Ecotravel.com

Whale watching is a popular ecotourism activity

Removing shoes before entering religious buildings is common practice in many countries

Ecotourism v responsible tourism

There is a certain amount of overlap between the terms ecotourism and responsible tourism, and to a certain extent the terms are interchangeable. However, perhaps one important difference is that, whereas the term 'ecotourist' could be used to describe someone who travels to certain destinations and takes part in ecotourism activities, it is possible for everyone to become more responsible tourists, even if they are visiting popular purpose-built resort destinations on a package holiday.

Every tourist is able to make a contribution to the process of sustainable tourism by behaving in a responsible manner when visiting a destination. These measures include:

● Learning about the country, through reading guidebooks, learning a few key terms of the language

Respecting signs is a simple way of being a responsible tourist

and obtaining information about local cultural attractions from tourist information centres;

- Being aware of appropriate cultural behaviour, such as respecting the dignity and privacy of others and dressing appropriately, especially in religious areas;

- Protecting plants and animals by not buying products made from endangered species and being especially careful when visiting sensitive areas by respecting all notices.

Buy local, eat local, stay local

The maxim of 'buy local, eat local and stay local' is a good example of how all tourists can act in a responsible manner and support sustainable tourism in destination areas. 'Buying local' means purchasing produce grown or reared locally from local producers rather than from supermarket chains. This helps to

reduce the number of 'food miles' as well as supporting businesses in the locality. 'Eating local' means eating in restaurants and cafés run and managed by local people as opposed to multinational chains. This will provide more employment and reduce the amount of 'leakage' from the local area. 'Staying local' refers to staying in locally-run and owned accommodation rather than in hotels owned by multinational companies or chains. Again, this will help keep more money in the locality and support the local community.

Supporting locally-managed tourism businesses is a good example of responsible tourism

Buying locally supports the local economy

The future of tourism

It is clear that there is now a greater awareness of the threat of climate change and of the wider issues facing the use of the Earth's resources. It has to be accepted that virtually all methods of travel create some form of impact on the environment. Although we can attempt to manage and reduce the impact of travel, it

There are many ways of reminding tourists how they can minimise their impact

is not possible, using present technology, to travel any distance without having some form of impact. So, what might happen in the near future? Will flights become more expensive so that less people can afford them, or will there be a maximum number of flights any person is allowed to take in a given period?

Alternatively, will technology develop new fuels that do not damage the environment or contribute to climate change? Will people visit more artificial destinations, such as the large-scale Eden Project structures with artificial beaches and recycled water?

The answer to these questions is not yet known, but there is an increasing awareness that everyone can make a contribution by making responsible decisions about where they travel, the activities they take part in, what they buy and where they stay, while they are enjoying themselves as tourists.

4.8 Change in travel and tourism

It will be clear to any reader that the world of travel and tourism is constantly changing and the organisations which make up the travel and tourism industry have to continually modify their operations in order to compete and survive as commercial enterprises. As we have just seen, the future of tourism could be said to be one of uncertainty in which rising costs of travel and the growing awareness of the negative impacts of tourism mean that leisure travel, as we know it today, may not exist in the same way in the future. On the other hand, the optimistic view would be that new technologies will be developed to provide a means of facilitating travel without causing significant damage to the environment or contributing to climate change.

Tiananmen Square, where hundreds of people were massacred less than twenty years ago, is now a tourist attraction for visitors to Beijing in China

143

Similarly, there may be additional barriers to travel imposed as a result of political actions. In recent years, new destinations have welcomed tourists. The 2008 Olympic Games held in Beijing symbolise the extent to which countries, which a few years ago were inaccessible, now see the value of hosting international events and the benefits of welcoming tourists. Perhaps political and other events in the near future will mean that some popular tourist destinations become much less safe to visit.

This last section summarises the changes that have taken place, and are still taking place, both within travel and tourism and in society in general. These changes can be summarised under the following headings:

- Socio-economic changes
- Technological changes
- Product development and innovation
- Changing customer needs, expectations and fashions

Socio-economic changes

Socio-economic changes were extremely important in the development of the travel and tourism industry during the twentieth century. Changing social conditions from the period immediately before the Second World War provided ordinary people with the time in which they could undertake leisure activities and the opportunity to travel to seaside resorts and other destinations. This was facilitated by the Holidays With Pay Act. At the same time, the development of the holiday camp concept gave many people their first tourism experience.

The major socio-economic factors that encouraged the growth of travel and tourism through the second half of the twentieth century have been identified as:

1. Increased amounts of time available for leisure, travel and tourism activities brought about by shorter working hours;
2. Increased amounts of disposable income for many people, which meant that they could afford a holiday and increasingly could afford more than one holiday each year;
3. Greater personal mobility as a result of increased car ownership and other transport developments;
4. Early retirement and increased life expectancy has meant that more people are taking part in tourism activities much later in their lives.

These trends continued throughout the second half of the twentieth century and are still significant today.

Many older people visit popular Mediterranean resorts out of season when the temperature is not as high and costs are lower

Industry Info...

'The credit crunch'

In the last quarter of 2007 concerns were raised about a possible economic recession in the United Kingdom, resulting from the likely increased costs of mortgages and more difficult economic conditions forecast for 2008.

If this proves to be the case, there will be impacts on the travel and tourism industry. Travel and tourism relies to a large extent on the amount of disposable income people have available. If people feel less well off, they are likely to book less holidays or spend less money on a holiday, perhaps booking a domestic as opposed to an outbound holiday. However, most people are reluctant to cancel their holiday altogether – getting away for a short period is seen as a necessity by many British people.

Technological changes

Technological changes can be sub-divided into:

1. Transport developments;
2. Changes in communications and information technology.

Transport developments have provided more people with the means to travel. The increase in car ownership was one component of this, as well as having more roads to travel on, more bridges and tunnels and so on – theses factors have all made more destinations accessible by road transport. Trains have become faster and now link more city centres directly, creating an alternative to air travel for short-haul journeys.

The Millau viaduct in southern France is the tallest bridge in the world and was opened in 2004

The second significant transport development has been the development of the jet aircraft, which has made it possible for tourists to access long-haul destinations in a matter of hours. As suggested earlier, the development of the jet aircraft took place during the period after the end of the Second World War and the resulting technology has been put to civilian use through the production of aircraft capable of carrying hundreds of passengers at hundreds of miles per hour.

Industry Info...

The Airbus A380

The world's largest passenger aircraft, the A380, began commercial operations in the autumn of 2007 with the first scheduled flight from Singapore to Sydney.

It is the first passenger aircraft to have two complete decks, although the Boeing 747 *Jumbo Jet* does have limited seating on an upper deck. The normal seating configuration for the A380 aircraft is 555 passengers, although it can accommodate up to 800, depending on the number of seats the airline wants to put into each class.

BAA (British Airports Authority), which operates London Heathrow Airport, has spent £450 million preparing to be able to handle passengers arriving on the A380 when the plane starts flying into London in 2008.

www.a380.singaporeair.com

Recent developments in aircraft technology have not concentrated on size and speed as much as minimising the environmental impacts of air travel. The most modern aircraft are more fuel-efficient than their predecessors, create less emissions, make less noise and are made of recyclable materials.

Developments in communications and information technology have brought about tremendous changes for the way in which travel products are made available to customers. The internet has made it possible for people to make bookings in a way that would not have been possible ten to fifteen years ago. Increasing numbers of people are confident about booking online and are being encouraged to do so by a new breed of travel and tourism organisations that have become established since the birth of the internet. Many airlines are now encouraging passengers to check-in online and print their boarding cards before they travel to the airport.

In addition, tourists can access far more information about the destinations they are travelling to and the facilities available before they travel. Increasingly, tourists can view online weather forecasts or access web-cams to learn about current conditions at the destination. In some instances, people may decide to visit a destination at very short notice if the weather there is favourable.

Winter sports enthusiasts may decide to visit a resort at short notice if the skiing conditions are good

Product development and innovation

There is no doubt that there has been a tremendous amount of product development and innovation over the last sixty years or so in the travel and tourism industry. Product development can be seen in two ways:

1. The development of new products, which also includes the introduction of new products or innovation;
2. The improvement of existing products to make them more attractive to existing customers.

Package holidays and holiday camps are two good examples of products that were innovations when they were first introduced, but have undergone significant development since. Although the Butlin's holiday camps of he 1930s were seen as luxurious at the time, they would seem very primitive by today's standards. The Butlin's product has been developed continuously from 1938 to 2008 and in most of these seventy years something new has been offered to customers. One advantage of this is that product development of this nature helps to develop customer loyalty. One of the services provided by Butlin's modern holiday resorts is the opportunity to book the next visit to Butlins before you leave!

Similarly, package holidays have undergone continuous development since they were first introduced more than fifty years ago. Package holidays now include far more options in terms of the type of destination, the standard of accommodation, the choice of flight times, choice of meal arrangements and so on. In fact, in order to compete, some traditional providers of package holidays

Industry Info...

Butlin's holiday resorts

The modern Butlins is very different from the original holiday camp concept, although most accommodation is still in chalets. After opening many holiday camps in the early years of the company's operation, Butlins now run three holiday resorts at Skegness in Lincolnshire, Minehead in Somerset and Bognor Regis in Sussex.

Customers have a choice of three grades of chalet, which can be rented on a self-catering or dinner, bed and breakfast basis. The chalets are well-appointed and the highest grade gold apartments include:

- Maid service;
- Widescreen TV;
- DVD/video player;
- 2nd TV in the bedroom;
- Personal safe;
- Hairdryer.

All of the above were certainly not available in the first generation of Butlin's holiday camps! Additionally, potential customers can see what they are booking through an online 360 degree panoramic view of a chalet via the internet.

www.butlinsonline.co.uk

are now offering customers the opportunity to book individual components of the holiday through them. This means that customers could book flights through a low-cost airline and book the accommodation through a tour operator.

The introduction of low-cost airlines is another example of innovation within the travel and tourism industry. These airlines broke new ground in selling airline seats direct to the public rather than through paying a commission to travel agents for selling seats on their behalf. Also, the low-cost airlines made it clear from the start what charge the company was making for the flight and how much the taxes and other charges would cost the passengers. This had not been the case up until that point.

The low-cost airline product has been continuously developed since its initial introduction. One example of this development has been in the complexity of

In recent years low-cost airlines have added Croatia to their list of destinations

the route networks on offer from the budget airlines. Ten years ago, Ryanair and easyJet served a very small number of destinations, but they have developed their product by offering greater numbers of destinations each year. Between them, Ryanair and easyJet each now have flights to nearly one hundred destinations.

Industry Info...

easyJet route network

One of the ways in which the low-cost airlines such as easyJet have developed their product is through the addition of more routes to their network, serving new destinations each year.

Routes that easyJet will be operating for the first time in 2008 include:

- Liverpool to Innsbruck (Austria) from January 8th
- Paris to Biarritz (France) from February 7th
- London Luton to Jersey from March 30th
- Lyon (France) to Venice (Italy) from April 4th

In fact, 26 new routes are scheduled to be offered between January 8th and May 17th 2008.

Another example of the development of the easyJet product is that there are now many flights between countries outside of the United Kingdom. The first route operated by easyJet was between London Luton and Glasgow, which commenced on November 10th 1995.

www.easyJet.com

Changing customer needs, expectations and fashions

Today's tourists are far more sophisticated than those who spent a week in pre-Second World War holiday camps over sixty years ago. Generally, people have travelled more and have higher expectations in terms of the quality of service they receive and facilities they expect from their accommodation. For example, sixty years ago, en-suite rooms were not commonly found in most hotels. Part of the hotel experience was the sharing of toilet and bathrooms with other guests. Today, the great majority of hotels have en-suite facilities and, in fact, the provision of these facilities is sometimes used to differentiate between a hotel and a guesthouse.

Part of the fascination of travel, especially for those tourists who were able to take package holidays for the first time in the 1960s and 1970s, was that they could emulate those they saw as more affluent people who could afford to travel. Many forms of transport, such as rail and cruise liners, were, and still are, based on a system of different classes of travel.

The need of customers to experience a lifestyle that they had not had the opportunity to do so before was very important in the development of the modern travel and tourism industry. Once people had begun to experience higher quality accommodation and facilities, they expected it every time, and their expectations continued to increase!

Not all tourists craved the quality products and up-market accommodation on offer. Over time, a range of different types of holiday have become fashionable, leading to the growth in winter sports, activity

Modern cruise liners have a range of accommodation types available, many offering outside cabins with a view

holidays, short breaks, camping holidays and similar products. Holiday destinations or activities become more or less fashionable, sometimes for no apparent reason. Examples of these changes would include the European cities of Prague and Budapest, which are now fashionable to visit, whereas some time ago, Venice or Milan might have been more popular. In winter sports resorts, snow boarding is now more fashionable amongst young people, while many older visitors still prefer skiing. Cuba and the Dominican Republic are now more fashionable destinations within the Caribbean area, whereas in the past Bermuda and Jamaica would have been more popular.

And in the future...?

We can be sure that there will always be a desire to travel and to visit different places. In recent years, we have seen the emergence of one of the most extreme forms of travel – space tourism!

So the motivation will always be there. What is less certain is the fate of the factors that allow people to travel widely. Will more people be able to afford to travel into space in the future, or will a changing climate and increasingly scarce resources make leisure travel less affordable and perhaps socially unacceptable? Many people today have had the opportunity to visit a variety of destinations from an early age. Significant numbers of young children from the United Kingdom have travelled extensively in Europe and visited the USA and other long-haul destinations. More people from India, China and other newly-industrialised countries now have the opportunity and desire to travel.

In the foreseeable future, despite the threat of increased costs and environmental change, the desire to travel is likely to continue, and the travel and tourism industry will continue to provide products that satisfy this desire. Perhaps the longer term is more difficult to predict.

Industry Info...

Virgin Galactic

Virgin Galactic will be the first company to offer commercial trips into space. These could start as early as 2009. Space tourists will pay $200,000 (approximately £100,000) for a two and a half hour trip into space. The launch and landing of the Virgin spacecraft will be from a facility in New Mexico, USA. In fact, the space tourists will be taken to a height of 100 kilometres (60 miles) above the earth's surface, just outside of the atmosphere. Passengers will be able to experience weightlessness and will be able to look down to see the curvature of the earth's surface below.

Sir Richard Branson and members of his family are planning to be amongst the first space tourists.

www.virgingalactic.com

There will always be a desire to experience different landscapes and cultures

Glossary

A

Accommodation providers	Organisations providing rooms and beds in which tourists stay overnight. Accommodation providers range from large international chains of hotels to family businesses providing bed and breakfast accommodation.
Activity holidays	Holidays where the participants spend a significant amount of time being involved in the same activity. This may be a particular sport or leisure activity.
Airbus A380	The world's largest commercial aircraft which came into service in 2007. The first A380s in service were operated by Singapore Airlines. www.a380singaporeair.com
Airlines	Airlines are commercial organisations aiming to make a profit by carrying passengers in aircraft from one airport to another, either domestically or internationally.
Airports	Airports provide facilities for aircraft to land and take-off (runways). They also enable passengers to check-in and board aircraft through terminals. Airports make money through landing charges and by selling retail space in terminals.
Alternative tourism	Alternative tourism is seen as the opposite of mass tourism. The term alternative tourism is often used in association with ecotourism and indicates an alternative to the tourism that is provided by large multinational companies.
Alton Towers	Alton Towers is a theme park in Staffordshire and is one of the most visited tourist attractions in the United Kingdom. The park is known for its range of 'white knuckle' rides. www.AltonTowers.com
Association of British Travel Agents (ABTA)	ABTA is the trade organisation representing the interests of travel agents and tour operators in the United Kingdom. www.abta.com
Attractions	Literally facilities that attract tourists to them. These can be natural or purpose-built. Other attractions, such as castles and cathedrals, were not built as such, but have become attractions over time.
Automobile Association (AA)	One of the major motoring organisations in the United Kingdom. The AA also provides information on accommodation. www.theaa.com
Avis	A major global car hire company with branches at all major airports. www.avis.com

B

Backpacker hostels	Budget accommodation provided mainly for young travellers. These hostels are found throughout the world in major cities. Accommodation is mainly in shared dormitories.
Beamish	Beamish is an open air 'living museum' located in the north of England. The museum recreates life as it was in the Great North in the 1800s and early 1900s. www.beamish.org.uk

Bed & breakfast	Accommodation, normally in a family home, when a set price is charged for the bedroom and breakfast the next morning. Many hotels also offer bed and breakfast rates.
Benidorm	A major resort on the Costa Blanca (white coast) of Spain. Benidorm is located about 45 kilometres north of Alicante and is protected by high mountains giving it a warm winter climate. Benidorm is associated with mass tourism and busy night life.
Big Pit	Big Pit is part of the National Museums of Wales as it is a former working coal mine. Visitors are taken round the mine and the working conditions in which coal was extracted are explained. www.museumwales.ac.uk
Billy Butlin	Entrepreneur who founded the Butlin's chain of holiday camps in the United Kingdom, the first of which opened in Skegness in 1936. www.butlinsonline.co.uk
Bird flu	A disease affecting chickens and other poultry, which results in the areas in which the outbreak occurs becoming less attractive to tourists.
Blackpool	One of the major seaside resorts in the United Kingdom, located on the Lancashire coast. www.visitblackpool.com
Blackpool Pleasure Beach	A major attraction within the seaside resort of Blackpool with over 120 rides and spectacular shows including the Pepsi Max Big One roller coaster. www.blackpoolpleasurebeach.com
Blue Badge Guides	Blue Badge is the highest tourist guiding qualification whose guides are trained and examined about their knowledge of the area in which they operate. Blue Badge Guides are usually hired for walking tours of cities or for coach tours. www.blue-badge-guides.com
Blue Flag Beach	Blue Flag status is awarded to beaches that meet strict criteria relating to water quality and environmental management. There are over 3,000 Blue Flag beaches throughout the world.
bmi	bmi is one of three full-service airlines in the United Kingdom, along with British Airways and Virgin Atlantic, offering long-haul flights to a range of destinations. The company also competes with British Airways on short-haul routes. www.flybmi.com
Boeing 747 *Jumbo Jet*	The 747 was the first wide-bodied jet aircraft and, until it was recently surpassed by the Airbus 380, was the largest commercial aircraft in the world. Over 1,000 planes have been produced since the 1970s. www.boeing.com
Bournemouth	Bournemouth is a large coastal resort on the south coast of England, famous for its pier and beach. The Bournemouth International Centre is a major facility located adjacent to the beaches. www.bournemouth.co.uk
Brighton	Brighton is often seen as the birthplace of British tourism since it was to Brighton that Victorian people came to enjoy the benefits of bathing in the sea. Brighton is located on the south coast of England in the county of Sussex and one of its most famous attractions is the Brighton Pavilion. www.tourism.brighton.co.uk
Bristol Zoo	One of the largest zoos in the United Kingdom, located on the outskirts of Bristol. www.bristolzoo.org.uk

British Airways	British Airways is the largest airline in the United Kingdom (and one of the largest in Europe) operating domestic, short-haul and long-haul flights to over 600 destinations. www.ba.com
British Motor Racing Grand Prix	One of the largest sporting events held in the United Kingdom each year, normally in July. The Grand Prix is a round of the Formula 1 World Drivers' Championship. www.silverstone.co.uk
British Museum	A major museum situated in central London with free admission. The museum has a wide range of temporary and permanent exhibitions. www.britishmuseum.org
'Bucket and spade'	The term used for traditional seaside family holidays where people would spend time on the beach building sandcastles.
Buckingham Palace	The Queen's London home, located close to Green Park and Westminster. The palace is open to the public at certain times of the year when the Queen is not in residence. www.royal.gov.uk
Budget	The amount of money available for a holiday. Also used to describe low-cost airlines, which generally provide cheaper travel than traditional 'full-service' airlines.
Budget hotel	A type of accommodation that has grown rapidly in recent years, a result of low prices, flexibility and convenience. Aimed at both leisure travellers and the business market, successful brands include Travelodge, Holiday Inn Express and Comfort Inn
Business travel	Business travel is defined as travelling away from home for business purposes, such as meetings, conferences or trade fairs. Business class is used to describe a class of travel which is more expensive and has more services.
'Buy local, eat local and stay local'	A maxim used to explain how eating and buying local produce and staying in locally-owned accommodation can benefit the communities in which tourism takes place and support sustainable tourism.

C

Camping	Sleeping in tents, normally on a recognised campsite.
Canadian Rockies	The mountainous area of western Canada famous for spectacular scenery and the winter resorts of Banff and Lake Louise amongst others.
Canal or river cruising	Holidays taken by hiring a canal boat or river cruiser normally sleeping between four and eight people.
Caravans	Touring caravans are towed behind cars and are used for accommodation on campsites. These caravans provide the owners with a choice as to where they can take the caravan. Static caravans (mobile homes) are found on campsites and cannot be moved, so are used as a second home by the owner or are often hired by commercial operators.
Center Parcs	Centre Parcs operate four family-orientated holiday villages in England. Each village is self-contained and offers a range of indoor and outdoor activities. www.centerparcs.com

Channel Tunnel	Opened to passenger and freight traffic in 1994, the Channel Tunnel runs beneath the Straits of Dover between Folkestone in England and Calais in France. Tourists can use the tunnel by the Eurostar train or by the shuttle trains that carry motor vehicles. www.eurotunnel.com
Charabancs	The name given to early forms of coaches, which were used for day trips to the seaside.
Charter flight	Charter flights are those operated by tour operators which have hired or chartered the aircraft to fly their package tour customers to their destination. The flight is not a regular or scheduled service.
Commercial	A commercial organisation operates in order to make a profit on the products and services it provides to customers. Virtually all the large organisations in the travel and tourism industry operate on a commercial basis.
Commission	Commission is a sum of money paid by a principal (such as an airline or tour operator) to a travel agent. This is usually a percentage of the value of the sale.
Computer reservation systems (CRS)	Computer systems that allow travel agents and the public to make online reservations with airlines, accommodation providers and tour operators.
Cross-channel ferry	Ferries crossing the English Channel between England and France. Most crossings are between the ports of Dover and Calais, although sailings also take place from Poole and Portsmouth. The three principal companies providing services across the Channel are P&O, Sea France and Brittany Ferries.
Cruise ships	Cruise ships (liners) are large 'floating hotels', which are used for holidays where the ships cruise from port to port, with stops at each, to allow passengers to visit the attractions nearby.
Cultural holidays	Holidays where the main purpose is to discover and enjoy aspects of the culture of the destination being visited. This may include food and drink, dance and festivals, museums and galleries or historic places and attractions.
Customer loyalty	A customer loyalty scheme is the concept whereby customers of a travel and tourism organisation choose to make bookings more than once over a period of time because the customers feel that they have received good service and value for money.

D

Department for Culture, Media and Sport (DCMS)	The government department of the United Kingdom responsible for leisure, tourism and related policies. www.dcms.gov.uk
Department for Environment, Food and Rural Affairs (DEFRA)	The government department of the United Kingdom responsible for countryside areas, as well as for sustainable policies. www.defra.gov.uk
Department for Transport	The government department responsible for all transport policies including airports, airlines, rail and road transport. www.dft.gov.uk

Disney	The American corporation with varied leisure and tourism interests, including theme parks in Florida, California, Hong Kong and Paris, as well as cruise ships and other products. www.disney.com
Domestic tourism	When people take holidays, short breaks and business trips in their own country. For example, a family from Worcester taking a two-week holiday in a caravan in Wales or a group of academics from London attending a conference in Sheffield are both examples of domestic tourism.
Duxford	Duxford, in Cambridgeshire, is one of the largest aviation museums in Europe. The site is part of the Imperial War Museum and has collections of tanks and military vehicles as well as aircraft. www.duxford.iwm.org.uk

E

easyJet	easyJet is one of the two major 'budget' or 'low-cost' airlines operating from a number of United Kingdom airports, flying to almost 100 destinations. www.easyjet.com
Economic leakage	Economic leakage involves the money spent by tourists at a destination not staying in that destination, but instead leaking out of the area. The term is usually applied to less economically developed countries (LEDCs), where money is spent in large hotels not owned by local people.
Ecotourism	Ecotourism is when the main purpose of travel is to appreciate the natural environment of an area or to learn more about its culture and natural history.
Eden Project	The Eden Project is one of the most successful visitor attractions in the United Kingdom. The project is located in a former clay quarry in Cornwall and consists of large plastic 'biomes' under which different climatic conditions and ecosystems have been created. www.edenproject.com
Euro	The currency adopted on 1st January 2002 as part of Economic and Monetary Union (EMU) by the following 12 countries: Austria, Germany, Luxembourg, Belgium, Greece, the Netherlands, Finland, Italy, Portugal, France, Ireland and Spain.
European Union	A grouping of 27 European countries, known as member states, which have joined together to safeguard peace and promote economic and social progress in Europe.
Eurostar	Eurostar is the high-speed train service that travels between London, Paris and Brussels using the Channel Tunnel. Since the Eurostar terminal moved to St Pancras station in London in November 2007, journey times between London and Paris have been reduced to 2 ¼ hours. www.eurostar.com
Exchange rates	Exchange rates refer to the relative value of one currency compared with another. As exchange rates change, it can become cheaper or more expensive when tourists visit another country.

Expedia	Expedia is an online travel company owned by airlines and other travel providers. Customers can book flights, hotels, car hire and other travel products using the internet. www.expedia.co.uk
External pressures	External (or outside) pressures that affect and cause change in the travel and tourism industry and over which the industry has no control.

F

Ferries	Ferries are ships and boats used to transport passengers and/or vehicles across bodies of water, which may be rivers or seas.
Five-star hotel	Five-star hotels are regarded as luxurious, exclusive and expensive, offering a wide range of services to guests.
Flag carriers	Airlines that would have been the major airline of their respective countries in the past, often supported by the government of the country. Examples include British Airways and Air France. Today, many flag carriers operate as commercial organisations.
Fly/cruise	The concept of flying to a port to start a cruise holiday, for example Miami in Florida, USA from where Caribbean cruises depart.
Foot and mouth disease	A disease affecting cattle of which there have been a number of outbreaks in different areas of the United Kingdom in recent years. Foot and mouth often results in a fall in tourist numbers to the region in which it is occurring.
Full-service	Name given to traditional airlines offering assigned seating and complimentary meals to distinguish them from the low-cost or budget carriers.

G

Global distribution systems (GDS)	The name sometimes used to describe the major computerised reservation systems (CRS) that have been developed by the world's biggest airlines, e.g. Sabre and Worldspan. The main feature of a GDS system is that it gives the user access to a wide range of related travel services, not just airline information.
Green tourism	Another form of ecotourism which is undertaken with a concern for the preservation of the environment and culture of the tourism destination.
Grey market	The term applied to people over the age of 50-55 who have a high level of disposable income and free time to spend taking holidays. This market has grown significantly as people live longer and enjoy active retirements.

H

Hertz	Hertz is one of the largest car hire companies in the world operating in all major cities and from all major airports. www.hertz.com

Hilton	A chain of four-star hotels found throughout the world. www.hilton.com
Holiday camps	A form of holiday accommodation developed in the early years of the twentieth century.
Holiday Inn Express	A budget brand of Holiday Inns with a smaller range of services. www.hiexpress.co.uk
Holidays	The general term used to describe periods spent away from home engaged in leisure and tourism activities.
Holidays with Pay Act (1938)	The Act of Parliament passed in 1938 that gave most workers in the United Kingdom the entitlement to one weeks paid holiday each year. Later Acts increased this entitlement.
Horizontal integration	Horizontal integration refers to mergers between organisations at the same level in the distribution chain, e.g. a large hotel company taking over a small independent hotel. Firms integrate horizontally to gain competitive advantage.

I

Independent holidays	Holidays organised by the people who are taking them as opposed to being bought as a package through a travel agent or tour operator. These are similar to self-packaged holidays.
Infrastructure	Refers to items such as airports, communications, roads, railways, water supply and sewage services, i.e. all those services that need to be in place before development of any kind, including leisure and tourism projects, can go ahead.
Ironbridge	Ironbridge Gorge Museum in Shropshire is a World Heritage Site built around the site of the world's first iron bridge. www.ironbridge.org.uk

J

Jorvik Viking Centre	A 'living museum' in York, northern England, which shows how Viking people lived in what is now central York over 1,000 years ago. www.jorvik-viking-centre.co.uk

K

Kinder Scout	Kinder Scout is an upland area of gritstone in the Dark Peak of Derbyshire. Mass protests on Kinder Scout led to the setting up of National Parks in the United Kingdom.

L

Landing charges	The main source of income for airports, which charge airlines for landing on the runway and making use of the airport facilities.
lastminute.com	One of the earliest and best-known online travel companies offering holidays, flights and other travel products via the internet. www.lastminute.com

Las Vegas	Las Vegas is located in the state of Nevada USA and is recognised as the gambling capital of the world. Large resort hotels also contain attractions and entertainment facilities. www.visitlasvegas.com
Living museums	Museums in which staff are dressed in costume and act as people who lived at the period of history in which the museum is set.
Long-haul	The term used to describe a flight lasting more than 4 or 5 hours. Generally these flights are to destinations outside of Europe.
Longleat	Longleat is a major visitor attraction in Wiltshire, which consists of a stately home as well as the first Safari Park in the United Kingdom. www.longleat.com
Los Angeles	Major city in California, USA containing the areas of Hollywood and Santa Monica. Other attractions include the Universal Studios theme park. www.lacity.org
Low-cost	Term used to describe 'budget' airlines as opposed to traditional or full-service airlines. easyJet and Ryanair are the most successful budget airlines in the United Kingdom.

M

Mass tourism	Mass tourism is the term used to describe large-scale tourism, mainly to coastal resorts in the Mediterranean area. Most mass tourism is developed by tour operators providing package holidays.
Megabus	Coach company offering scheduled, budget coach travel between major cities in the United Kingdom. www.megabus.com
Multiple	A travel company that has many branches located throughout the UK. Many multiples are household names in the travel industry, such as Thomas Cook and My Travel, and are sometimes part of large parent organisations.
Multiplier effect	The term used to describe the way in which tourism expenditure affects the local community by creating further spending, thus multiplying the initial spending.

N

National Express	National Express is a coach and train operating company providing a range of scheduled services between major towns and cities in the United Kingdom. www.nationalexpress.com
National Parks	National Parks are protected areas containing spectacular scenery and valued landscapes. There are 14 national parks in the United Kingdom, the first of which were established over 50 years ago. National Parks are found in most countries. www.nationalparks.gov.uk
National Trust	The National Trust is a voluntary organisation. The Trust looks after about 350 historic houses, gardens, industrial monuments and mills which are open to the public. www.nationaltrust.org.uk

Natural attraction	The term used to identify natural as opposed to purpose-built visitor attractions. Many people want to visit spectacular waterfalls, mountain landscapes, cliffs and other coastal landforms or forest areas – these are all natural attractions.
Network Rail	Network Rail is the company that owns and maintains the railway tracks in the United Kingdom. It also owns and operates 18 key railway stations. Train operating companies (TOCs) run the trains on the track owned by Network Rail. www.networkrail.co.uk
Niagara Falls	Niagara Falls lie on the border between Canada and the USA and are one of the most spectacular waterfalls in the world. www.niagarafallstourism.com
Niche market	The term used to describe small numbers of tourists with particular needs which are provided for by specialist tour operators.
Notting Hill Carnival	One of the largest events to take place on an annual basis in the United Kingdom. The carnival takes place over the August Bank Holiday weekend in west London and celebrates Afro-Caribbean culture in particular.

O

Oakwood	Oakwood is a theme park located in Pembrokeshire, south west Wales. www.oakwoodthemepark.co.uk
Olympic Games	The Olympic Games are a major sporting event held every four years. The Olympics generate significant amounts of inbound tourism for the countries and cities hosting the Games. www.olympic.org
Online check-in	The process whereby passengers can check-in for a flight by accessing the website of the airline they are travelling with and printing out a boarding pass. This is an advantage for passengers travelling with cabin luggage only.
Open skies	Open skies is the policy of governments allowing airlines from different countries to operate over a country's airspace, thus creating more competition between carriers.
Opodo	Opodo is an online travel organisation providing a range of travel products. www.opodo.com
Orlando	A town in central Florida USA, around which the major Disney and Universal Studios resorts and theme parks are located. www.orlandoinfo.com
Outbound tourism	The term used for people travelling out of the country in which they live for tourism purposes.
Over-dependency	Over-dependency occurs when a destination relies too much on tourism for its income and employment. A downturn in tourist numbers might create difficult economic conditions in these areas.

P

Package holiday	An all-inclusive holiday, sometimes referred to as a package tour or inclusive tour (IT), which normally consists of three components – travel, accommodation and transfer services.
Park and ride	Schemes that operate in a number of historic cities and some National Parks. They encourage visitors not to drive into city centres by building large car parks at the edge of the city with buses provided to take visitors into central areas.
Peak District National Park	The Peak District in Derbyshire was the first National Park to be designated in the United Kingdom. It is also one of the most visited National Parks, with the cities of Manchester and Sheffield within easy reach. www.peakdistrict.org
Principal	The term principal is given to travel companies and accommodation providers, from which tour operators buy products to create package holidays.
Private	The term private, as in private sector, is used to identify commercial organisations that exist to make a profit.
Products	Products are what customers buy. Many products of the travel and tourism industry are seen as intangible products, which cannot be physically touched. Holidays are one of the main products of the industry.
Public	The term public, as in public sector, is used to identify public sector organisations that are funded by national or local government and do not have to make a profit through the sale of their products.
Purpose-built	Purpose-built, as opposed to natural visitor attractions, are built with the purpose of attracting tourists to them and, in the majority of cases, organisations aim to make a profit through charging visitors to enter the attractions. Theme parks would be an example of purpose-built attractions.

R

RCI	Resort Condominiums International is a company specialising in exchange holidays for people who own timeshares all over the world. www.rci.com
Resort	A resort is a village or town in which the main function is tourism. The resort will contain a significant amount of accommodation and other tourist facilities. The term is often used to identify ski resorts and coastal resorts. In North America, the term 'resort' can also be used to describe a hotel and leisure complex.
Responsible tourism	Responsible tourism is about encouraging tourists to respect the environment and culture of the tourist area they are visiting by 'buying local, eating local and staying local'.
Retailer	A retailer sells the products of wholesalers to the public. Within the travel industry, travel agents are seen as retailers and tour operators as wholesalers.
Roll-on-roll-off (RORO)	RO-RO is a term used to describe vehicle ferries where vehicles can be loaded at one end of the vessel and they can drive off without turning round.

Ryanair	Ryanair is one of the most successful budget or no-frills airlines, whose profits and passenger numbers have grown significantly over the last decade. www.ryanair.com

S

Scarborough	Scarborough is an important seaside town on the Yorkshire coast. www.scarborough.gov.uk
Scheduled	Scheduled flights are offered by airlines that operate at advertised set times to set destinations, regardless of the demand.
Seasonal employment	Seasonal employment refers to jobs which do not exist all year round, but are only available when there is a demand for them because of the number of tourists visiting an area. Jobs in some hotels, campsites, ski resorts and attractions are seasonal.
Self check-in	A system where airline passengers check-in using electronic equipment at the airport rather than at a check-in desk.
Self-drive	A tourism trip where the main form of transport is a family car or hire car. One or more members of the party drive the vehicle.
Self-packaging	The type of tourist trip where members of the party make flight, accommodation and other bookings, rather than using the services of a travel agent.
Serviced	The term serviced applies to accommodation which is cleaned and 'serviced' by staff working for the accommodation provider. This usually happens on a daily basis.
Shearings	Shearings is one of the largest companies offering coach tour holidays within the United Kingdom – it is a domestic tour operator. www.shearings.com
Short breaks	Holidays generally lasting two to four nights. These are often taken as a second holiday in the year.
Sir Freddie Laker	Entrepreneur who offered cheap flights to the USA in competition with the major airlines. Sir Freddy heralded the way for other low-cost or budget airlines.
Skytrain	The first transatlantic passenger air service operated by Sir Freddie Laker. The service commenced in 1971 and flew between Gatwick Airport and JFK Airport in New York.
Small to medium-sized enterprises (SMEs)	Small and medium-sized businesses, which may only employ a few people or family members, are found throughout the travel and tourism industry, such as small attractions and certain types of accommodation.
Special interest holidays	A holiday where a significant amount of time is spent taking part in a particular activity, normally by a group of people who all have the same interest. This could involve painting, bird-watching, wine-tasting or a range of similar activities.
Sporting holidays	A form of special interest holidays which are taken (often as short breaks) to participate in, or watch, sporting activities. Golf holidays or visits to watch international rugby events are examples.

Sunlust	The notion that certain people wish to spend their holiday time enjoying the sun and seek destinations where long hours of sunshine are guaranteed.
Support services	Support services are those organisations such as tourist boards and tourist information centres, which offer support to commercial organisations providing travel and tourism products.
Sustainable tourism	Essentially, sustainable tourism is about meeting the needs of today's tourists without causing adverse effects on the environment or community in which the tourism is taking place.

T

Thomas Cook	Thomas Cook is seen as the founder of package holidays who began organising tours in 1841. Today Thomas Cook is a major tour operator and provider of a range of holiday products. www.thomascook.co.uk
Thomson (TUI)	A major provider of travel products in the United Kingdom offering holidays, flights, cruises and hotel reservations. www.thomson.co.uk
Thorpe Park	Thorpe Park is a major visitor attraction in Surrey, to the west of London. The theme park has seen the development of a number of 'white knuckle' rides in recent years. www.thorpepark.com
Ticketless	Quite literally, no printed ticket is issued by the company providing travel, which may be a flight, rail or other journey. The passenger is allowed to travel on production of a reference number indicating that they have purchased the journey.
Tourism	Tourism is defined by the World Tourism Organisation (WTO) as '...the activities of persons travelling to and staying in places outside their usual environment for not more than one consecutive year for leisure, business and other purposes'.
Tourism Alliance	The Tourism Alliance is a group of organisations and companies with an interest in tourism, which exists to lobby government about matters relating to the industry. www.tourismalliance.com
Tourism Society	The Tourism Society is a professional membership body for people working in all sectors of the travel and tourism industry. www.tourismsociety.org
Tour operator	Tour operators assemble inclusive tours by buying components such as flights and accommodation (from principals) and selling them as a complete package, either directly to the public or through a travel agent.
Train operating companies (TOCs)	A group of private sector companies providing scheduled rail services in the United Kingdom.
Transport providers	Companies, and in some cases local authorities, offering transport services for tourists.

Travelocity	Online travel company providing bookings for holidays, flights, accommodation and car hire. www.travelocity.co.uk
Travelodge	A chain of lodge accommodation that operates throughout the United Kingdom. Travelodge provides standard en-suite rooms for up to four people in locations adjacent to motorway junctions and on major roads. www.travelodge.co.uk
Travel agent	Travel agents traditionally sell the products of tour operators and other providers of travel products such as airlines and accommodation providers. Travel agents also sell travel insurance and provide currency exchange. They make a commission on the sale of these products.
Travel Counsellors	Travel Counsellors was established in 1994 and all of its agents work from home rather than in high-street travel agencies. The agents are linked by the internet to the company's head office. www.travelcounsellors.co.uk

U

Universal Studios	Universal Studios operate a number of theme parks in the USA, notably in Los Angeles and Florida. Many rides and attractions are themed around films and TV programmes produced by the studios. Universal Studios also operate Port Aventura in Spain. www.universalstudios.com
Unserviced	The term applied to accommodation which is not cleaned or 'serviced' by staff at the accommodation. It is the responsibility of the person hiring the accommodation to undertake this. Holiday cottages, apartments and villas are often, but not always, unserviced.

V

Vertical integration	A process whereby companies at different levels of the distribution chain are linked in some way to give competitive advantage. For example, Thomson, the UK's number one tour operator, owns the thomsonfly airline, while Club 18-30 Holidays is part of the Thomas Cook Group. By working together, the companies hope to secure increased sales, thereby improving their market share.
Virgin Atlantic	Virgin Atlantic is one of three major airlines based in the United Kingdom which offer transatlantic and other long-haul flights. The others are British Midland and British Airways. www.virgin-atlantic.com
VisitBritain	VisitBritain is the body responsible for promoting inbound tourism to the United Kingdom and travel within England by people living in the UK. www.visitbritain.org
Visiting friends and relatives (VFR)	Visiting friends and relatives is seen as one of the three main reasons for tourism, the others being for leisure and business reasons.
Voluntary sector	Voluntary organisations provide a range of products and services within the tourism industry, but do not aim to make a profit from their activities. Examples include the National Trust and the Youth Hostels Association.

W

Wanderlust

Wanderlust refers to the desire to travel, to see different places and to experience different cultures.

Wholesaler

Within the travel industry the wholesaler is seen as the tour operator, which produces a range of package holiday products that are sold to the public through retailers – travel agents.

World Tourism Organisation

The World Tourism Organisation is an agency of the United Nations. The WTO plays a vital role in promoting the development of responsible and sustainable tourism, paying particular attention to the interests of developing countries. www.unwto.org

Y

Youth Hostels Association

One of the largest providers of accommodation in the United Kingdom. The YHA operates as a charity and offers budget hostel accommodation in a range of city and countryside areas. YHA members receive a discount on the costs. www.yha.org.uk

Z

Zermatt

Traditional traffic-free ski resort in Switzerland, reached by rail rather than road. www.zermatt.ch

Zoom

A low-cost or budget airline operating routes from the United Kingdom to cities in the USA and Canada. www.flyzoom.com

Index